Composting

SMITH & HAWKEN

The Hands · On Gardener

Composting

by LIZ BALL

with illustrations

by JIM ANDERSON

WORKMAN PUBLISHING · NEW YORK

To Rick, especially, for his support, advice and patience.
To Sarah, for her understanding that I could not spend the time
with her that I hoped to while this book was in progress.

Over the last fifteen years I have become increasingly devoted to
gardening and to writing about it. In that time, I've also become
aware of how easy it is to take soil for granted, or worse, inadvertently
harm it. Writing about how to participate in building and maintaining
rich, fertile soil in the backyard by means of composting was something that I was eager to do. Special thanks to Jeff Ball for leading the
way in this and many, many other things; and to John Meils at Workman Publishing and Bonnie Dahan at Smith & Hawken for their guid-
ance. I am also indebted to innumerable composting friends and
garden writer colleagues, particularly Cyane Gresham and Rodale
Institute, who have educated me in the techniques, benefits and, yes,
even joys of composting.

Published simultaneously in Canada by Thomas Allen & Son Limited.

Library of Congress Cataloging-in-Publication Data
Ball, Liz.
Composting / by Liz Ball; illustrations by Jim Anderson.
p. cm.—(Smith & Hawken—the hands-on gardener)
Includes index.
ISBN 0-7611-0732-0
1. Compost.
I. Title. II. Series.
S661.B355 1998
635'.048975—dc21   97-32748
CIP

Workman Publishing Company
708 Broadway, New York, NY 10003-9555

Manufactured in the United States of America

First printing January 1998
10 9 8 7 6 5 4 3 2 1

CONTENTS

A COMPOSTING PRIMER

A garden is only as healthy as its soil. Regardless of a plant's beauty or suitability to the garden, it's success ultimately depends on the nourishing capability of the soil. Experienced gardeners have learned that the most important gardening work—building soil that is fertile, well-draining, and absorbent—takes place before anything is planted. And the best way to prepare soil is by adding compost to it every year.

In part a science, but mostly an art, composting can be a very rewarding activity. By fostering the natural cycle whereby organic materials are transposed into rich humus, gardeners improve their gardens, recycle yard waste, and reduce pest and disease problems. They save money on fertilizers, topdressings, water, and pesticides. And the best part is that composting is easy to do and will happen whether you intervene in the process or not.

Even a minimal understanding of composting reveals that it's a very logical, easy process, one that has been practiced in different forms throughout history. And your involvement in composting can be minimal or extensive, depending on your needs and time. The following pages will present an array of composting options, from simply piling organic debris and letting Nature do the work to managing a series of piles for a larger amount of compost.

FROM MANURE TO MANAGED COMPOST: AN AGRICULTURAL CONTINUUM

The history of home composting is intertwined with development of agriculture as a whole. Observing the natural decomposition of organic material on the forest floor, in meadows, and along the water's edge, prehistoric farmers sought to duplicate the process by deliberately piling mixtures of animal manure, plant debris, and soil in hope of promoting its decomposition. The resulting product—called compost or humus—is still the primary source of soil nutrients in many parts of the world, despite the prevalence of manufactured fertilizer products.

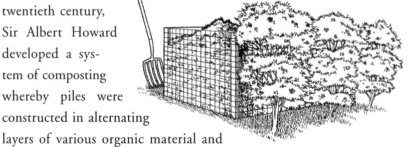

In the early twentieth century, Sir Albert Howard developed a system of composting whereby piles were constructed in alternating layers of various organic material and manure. Howard deduced that decomposition was most efficient when when the ratio of plant material to manure was three to one. Later in this century, composting was adopted by serious gardeners, especially those who followed the organic principles popularized by the Rodale family.

The advent of the environmental movement in the 1960s helped introduce composting to a broad segment of the population, including industry, commercial enterprises, municipalities, and nongardening households. Suddenly, composting became an easy way to reduce the pressure on overburdened landfills and practice environmental responsibility. The lawn and garden industry responded to the surging interest in composting by developing a host of new products that do everything from aerating a compost pile to practically turning it for you.

DO IT YOUR WAY

Because decomposition of dead and discarded organic materials is a natural process, it's very easy to make compost. When the essentials—air, moisture, carbon, and nitrogen—are present, it's virtually automatic. Therefore, the degree of your involvement in composting is extremely flexible.

Some gardeners simply want to avoid adding to the municipal waste stream and will pile their organic debris haphazardly and let Nature take its course. These people are more than happy harvesting a few bushels of compost each year from their "simple" compost pile. Others are more serious about the process and will "manage" a composting system, assuring quick decomposition and bushels of humus. These gardeners typically chop or shred materials for piles, or fill bins, roll tumblers, make compost "tea," or employ the services of worms. The truly obsessed do all of these things. Most gardeners, however, fall somewhere in between the two extremes.

The smart gardener is prepared for the possibility that a modest composting project may become increasingly more intensive over the years. Compost is such a valuable, useful product that you may become impatient to add more piles, and employ different ways to speed the decomposition process. This will yield more material for your garden beds, houseplants, shrubs, trees, and lawn.

GETTING STARTED

This primer will introduce you to the art and science of composting, plus help you begin your own backyard composting project. In the following pages, you'll find information on every aspect of the process, from where to site your pile to using compost most efficiently. The information will help you make initial decisions about how deeply you want to get involved in composting, and what you'll need to do it.

Begin by assuming that your soil needs improvement. Typically, soil in most residential yards is compacted and depleted of organic matter.

While it's a good idea to pinpoint specific areas of soil that need improvement—so that you can estimate how much compost you'll need—there's nothing wrong with just starting in. Your efforts will be limited, to some extent, by how much organic material you generate in your yard, but seasoned gardeners quickly learn how to forage from other places. If you're lucky enough to have trees on your property, then you already have a wonderful source of leaves, the backbone of most backyard composting operations.

Space is another critical consideration when starting a composting project. The more compost you intend to make, the more space you'll need for your pile. You'll also want to consider planning additional space for storing raw materials and tools. Storage of tools becomes especially important if you expect to move beyond the few basic tools: a cart, composting fork, shovel, and pruners. Shredding or chipping equipment can be quite large, and will therefore require adequate space for safe operation, as well as storage.

The sooner you can harvest compost and add it to your soil, the sooner your soil will be able to serve your plants. For those who intend to manage their composting process and reap compost quicker, there are lots of methods and products specifically designed to speed decomposition. While most are not necessary, some are quite helpful. Take time to evaluate these products carefully before buying any of them.

As you add compost, you add fertility to the soil. The microbial life in organic matter, or humus, converts other soil elements into essential nutrients that plants need. Fibrous humus also adds texture to your soil, and preserves precious air spaces for plant roots. Lastly, you add appropriate moisture to soil because the spongy humus absorbs and retains moisture for plants, while simultaneously draining excess away from plant roots.

Expect your composting system to change over time as you gain experience and find ever more uses for the wonderful compost that you produce. This book can help you every step of the way. Use it as a resource to dip into from time to time or as a texbook to be read through from start to finish.

WHAT IS SOIL?

The importance of soil is often overlooked in the grand scheme of the home gardener. Garden plans are drawn and implemented. Harvests are made year after year. All the while, precious little thought is given to the soil that makes it all possible. Not until plants become fraught with disease or vegetable yields decrease consistently is the question posed: How important is the health of my soil?

Learning about soil—its composition, health, and productivity—is the single most important thing to do when starting and maintaining a garden. It's easy to ascribe problems solely to other factors, such as light, water, pests, or finicky plants, but the truth is almost always figuratively written in the dirt. Soil that is rich with productive nutrients can help overcome a host of other deficiencies. Soil is not an inert substance; it requires regular feeding if you expect to reap its rewards.

Soil is made up of air, moisture, tiny particles of rock, and flecks of organic material. A handful of typical soil contains mostly inert, or non-living, substances. Only a very small proportion is living, or organic, matter. This organic matter, sometimes called humus, is literally the active ingredient that transforms what is essentially "dead" sterile dirt into "live" fertile soil.

The small amount of organic material that is in soil teems with life. Living organisms—as they feed and reproduce—accelerate the decomposition of the decaying leaves, grass clippings, or dying plants until they are no longer recognizable. They become a new substance—spongy, dark humus. It's naturally produced wherever there are sufficient organic materials, organisms, air, and moisture. When you purposely produce humus in your backyard from accumulated organic materials, you get compost.

THE LIFE OF SOIL

Whether it's called humus, compost, or decomposed organic matter, this small component of typical soil is extremely valuable and useful for growing plants. The presence of compost converts soil from simply a medium to support plants into a nurturing element that provides plants with the fuel and protection to thrive. The more humus present in the soil (3% to 5% is ideal), the richer it is in nutrients and the better it holds moisture and air for plant roots. The humus in soil also protects it against some of the harsh conditions that often prevail in typical soil.

Acting as a glue to hold inorganic particles together, humus helps retain moisture. Typical humus adds some nitrogen, phosphorus, potassium, and sulfur to infertile soils. It also attracts and holds nutrients and trace elements that might otherwise leach down through the soil in heavy rains. Some parts of humus become substances that stimulate plant growth and help defend against pests and diseases. This occurs because decomposed matter contains organisms that kill plant pathogens, which are toxins released into plants from various microorganisms.

Humus is so versatile because it harbors an incredible variety of both micro- and macroorganisms. These organisms break down the organic material, refine it, and convert its chemical components (nitrogen, calcium, phosphorus, potassium, and others) into a form that living plants can easily take up through their roots.

An incredible variety of bacteria, fungi, and other microbes we cannot see are found in humus. There are also visible organisms such as earthworms and sowbugs, among others. The microscopic organisms live mostly in the film of water that coats soil particles. The larger ones live in the air spaces between soil particles and break down bits of rock as they feed and reproduce, releasing their minerals and leaving them in a form easily digestible to plants.

MAKING HUMUS BY COMPOSTING

Most experienced gardeners are well aware of the relationship between the amount of organic matter in the soil and the health of their plants. Since time immemorial, gardeners have enriched their soil with humus in hopes of improving the size of their harvests. Early gardeners observed the natural process of organic decomposition in Nature and replicated it in their yards.

The history of backyard composting has been a story of gardeners' and farmers' efforts to perfect a method that intentionally creates humus from accumulated organic matter. Since gardeners have always been impatient, they have created methods for speeding up the decomposition process. Generations of gardeners' experimentation has yielded lots of shortcuts, techniques, and tools to hurry the process along. Regardless of the method, however, compost is always created in the same way—a range of microorganisms systematically decompose organic matter in a series of stages.

In simple terms, the composting process is fueled by the activity of numerous tiny organisms already in any pile of organic matter. Utilizing carbon and nitrogen, the microorganisms generate by-products that become the food source for yet another type of organism. Organic material undergoes progressive decomposition as it moves through this elaborate food chain. A succession of different types of microbes are involved until most of the biodegradable material is consumed and transformed. The remaining substance is the dark brown or black humus material called compost.

THE ACTUAL DECOMPOSITION PROCESS: The first job of home composting is to create a suitable environment for the microorganisms that decompose organic materials. While this happens continuously in Nature, it takes some preparation in the home landscape. This is particularly true if you want to speed the process. Microorganisms that are expected to work overtime need special care and feeding, and building a compost pile correctly is a big part of the process.

To understand how decomposition happens, it's important to know that microorganisms need some carbon-containing materials (brown), such as dried leaves or straw, and some nitrogen-containing materials (green), such as fresh grass clippings, weeds, or kitchen garbage. They also need oxygen and sufficient, but not excessive, moisture. These four ingredients—carbon, nitrogen, oxygen, and water—are the basics of successful composting.

Natural decomposition of organic materials takes place in five phases: oxidation, reduction, degradation, conversion, and maturation. Whether it takes place on the forest floor or in your backyard, decomposition always goes through these steps.

OXIDATION PHASE: Chemical oxidation from exposure to air and water starts automatically while substances wait to be deposited in a pile or bin. The activity of psychrophilic (cool temperature) bacteria begins to change the chemical state of materials as they start to digest carbon compounds.

REDUCTION PHASE: Decomposition is stimulated when insects, worms, and even humans begin to break down organic material into smaller pieces. Chopping or shredding the material before it goes into the pile exposes more surface area to oxidation. Mesophilic (medium temperature) bacteria are already beginning to eat and reduce the overall pile during this stage. Once decomposition advances enough for the pile to heat up, invertebrate worms, springtails, and mites head for the outside of the pile to escape the heat.

DEGRADATION PHASE: Simply put, the degradation phase involves microorganisms consuming protein and carbohydrates found in the waste material. As the microorganisms multiply and grow, they create energy in the form of heat, water, and carbon dioxide (CO_2). Decomposition moves into full swing as thermophilic (heat-loving) bacteria begin to replace mesophilic bacteria.

Fungus and actinomycetes, which are bacteria similar to mold, multiply and are consumed by other microorganisms, whose burgeoning population is encouraged by the rising temperature within the compost pile. When they have lots of air and moisture—an optimum environment—the thermophilic bacteria become so active that, in large piles, the temperature rises to a point where viruses and weed seeds are killed. In this phase, anaerobic microorganisms—bacteria that exist without oxygen—show up in piles that are not turned.

TEMPERATURE FLUCTUATIONS OF THE COMPOST PILE

Temperature	55°F	65°F	75°F	85°F	95°F	105°F	115°F	125°F	135°F	145°F	155°F
PHASES OF DECOMPOSITION											
OXIDATION ⇩	■										
REDUCTION ⇩		■									
DEGRADATION ⇩				■	■	■	■	■	■	■	
CONVERSION ⇩		■	■	■	■	■	■	■	■	■	
MATURATION	▌										
ORGANISMS THAT OCCUPY THE PILE AT DIFFERENT TEMPERATURES											
PYSCHROPHILES	■	■									
MESOPHILES			■	■							
THERMOPHILES					■	■	■	■	■	■	

CONVERSION PHASE: As the temperature drops in the pile, decomposition activity winds down. Other bacteria and fungi take over to complete the process. In this form, the compost is considered to be "fresh" or "raw." Decomposition will continue if the pile is left alone, but the conversion of organic materials into compost is essentially done. If the fresh compost is put into the soil, it will use some of the nitrogen already present in the ground for final decomposition. Thus, fresh compost is not considered as valuable as what is called "aged" or "mature" compost, where the decomposition process has all but ceased.

Turning compost regularly increases the rate of decomposition.

MATURATION PHASE: Recently decomposed organic matter ages, or cures, changing from "fresh" to "aged" compost. At this point, intense bacterial activity subsides, the pile cools down, and earthworms, springtails, and mites gradually return. The humus, or compost, is of optimum value at this time. However, the longer it sits around, the less nitrogen it will retain. This stage is especially important when making "active" or "fresh" compost (see page 77) because you'll want to harvest it at just the right time.

THE FINISHED PRODUCT: What's left after the breakdown of the organic materials is largely cells and skeletons of all the microorganisms that participated in the decomposing process; partially decomposed particles of organic matter (cellulose and lignin); and inorganic particles including glass, sand, rock, and other mineral elements that were on the surfaces of the organic material or were caught up in the pile. Some nutrients essential to plant growth are also present.

The actual amounts of various nutrients and trace minerals in compost vary from pile to pile. Nutrient content is largely determined by the type and proportions of carbon and nitrogen ingredients in the initial mix of organic material.

How the compost was made also factors into the nutrient equation. For instance, compost that was turned often—and therefore decomposed at a high heat because of exposure to air—usually has slightly more nitrogen than compost produced by a more passive method. However, the differences of nitrogen in the finished product have no practical significance for your plants and soil.

While compost is not dense enough in nutrients to substitute for fertilizer where soil is poor, adding it to your soil improves nutritional content over the long term. Gradually, your soil will be better able to support the microscopic life that keeps it healthy. The presence of individual nutrients in compost also helps to feed the plants themselves.

One concern of many gardeners and backyard compost enthusiasts is whether or not the addition of compost to their soil will change its pH, the level of acidity or alkalinity. Their suspicion is that the acidity of the original organic materials (for example, pine needles or oak leaves) will be reflected in the resulting compost. In fact, thanks to the activity

A COMPOSTING VIVARIUM

The decomposition process that takes place in your backyard compost pile can be simulated in a vivarium—an enclosure for keeping, raising, and observing animal life indoors. Using a common aquarium, you can create a "pet tank" to house a miniature ecosystem, or a mini-composter, with live shredders—the insects. Observing them through the glass as they go about their business is one of the simplest ways to understand how compost is made.

In the tank, you must create an environment with the four basic ingredients: air, moisture, carbon, and nitrogen. Collect damp, coarse organic matter, such as sticks, branches, and leaves, and cover them with soil or finished compost over half of the tank's bottom. Naturally occurring microbial life will already be on these materials. In addition, populate the tank with insects commonly found in compost piles or on forest floors—like earthworms, sowbugs, millipedes, spiders, slugs, and so on. Make sure the top of the tank is covered with fine wire mesh.

The tank also needs sunlight, but a fluorescent fish-tank light will suffice. The decomposition process will occur faster if the tank is hot, but maintain at least household temperature.

This composting vivarium will actually create small amounts of compost. You can place small plants in the tank for decoration, but make sure there is an open water source to provide humidity.

of earthworms, the pH level of most compost made with a variety of common backyard organic materials is close to neutral—registering from 6.8 to 7.2 on the pH scale.

The best way to manage pH is by using a variety of materials to make compost. If your plants are doing well, then the compost produced from their waste will be good for improving that soil. Until more research is done to prove the effect of compost on pH levels, you can accept the general fact that people who use lots of homemade compost always have good soil and healthy plants.

THE FINAL ANALYSIS: In many ways compost is still an unexplored frontier. Even after centuries of experimentation and study by farmers,

ACID ALERT

One of the potential components of compost is what scientists call fatty acids. Fatty acids are used in certain insecticides (for example, insecticidal soap) to control small, soft-bodied pest insects such as aphids, mites, and whiteflies. Depending on the materials used to make compost, the final compost product may have some of these fatty acids. Their presence may explain why compost seems to improve soil infested with disease pathogens. It has long been observed by gar-deners that planting bed soils amended with lots of compost tend to have fewer insect prob-lems than garden soils without it.

A substance called humic acid also typically shows up in fin-ished compost. It is valuable for conditioning heavy clay soils by making them lighter and helping them drain better. Humic acid also plays a special role in soils that may contain a large amount of aluminum. It binds with the aluminum to render it relatively inactive.

scientists, and gardeners worldwide, there is much that we don't know about how compost is made and how it encourages life in the soil. We do know, however, that compost is the key to abundant crops.

NURTURING
the SOIL

Where Nature is undisturbed, compost happens naturally. If you dig down below the ground cover of fallen leaves or brush, you'll likely find a crumbly layer of brown or black soil known as humus or compost. As plants die, they naturally decompose with the help of various insects and micro-organisms to help build the soil and support new plant life. This soil "cycle" is a constant in forests untouched by human hands.

In most American yards, however, the soil cycle is rudely interrupted on a regular basis. The organic materials naturally generated on the property are ignored or, worse yet, routinely discarded. Instead of allowing leaves and grass clippings to decompose and then return to the soil, many homeowners still bag them and put them out for trash. Weeds, prunings, and other organic debris—all beneficial to the soil once decomposed— are also regularly removed from the landscape permanently.

Once you begin to think about composting, all the organic materials in the yard become valuable. Leaves, dead plants, weeds, rotting stumps, sod, and bark take on new importance as potential sources of carbon or nitrogen to fuel the composting process. You can even take advantage of other sources of organic materials beyond your own yard.

Organic Materials for Composting

Organic materials are substances derived from living organisms, such as wood, as opposed to inorganic substances, such as rocks. These materials are made up of carbon and they biodegrade, or rot, over time in the presence of oxygen. For the purposes of composting, organic raw materials are most often plant-based waste or debris from the yard and garden.

Some of these materials are green and relatively soft, like grass clippings and fresh weeds. They contain a large amount of nitrogen and moisture. Others are brown and dried, like woody vines, fallen leaves, twigs, and bark, all of which contain carbon. Organic materials may also be processed substances derived from plants, like paper or used coffee grounds. They can also be animal matter such as meat and bones. In most cases, however, animal-based materials are not appropriate for backyard compost piles and can cause problems.

No matter what organic materials are used in composting, each substance contributes some basic nutrients. Nitrogen (N), phosphorus (P), and potassium (K) are the three primary plant nutrients. While much of the nitrogen is consumed during the decomposition process, the phosphorus and potassium—in some form—end up in the final product. They are not abundant enough to substitute for fertilizer, but they do provide some nutrition to plants. The relative amount of these three plant nutrients are called NPK levels.

Materials from the Yard: Most residences have enough organic materials for composting to serve the needs of all their plants, shrubs, and trees. There is often a near-perfect balance between the amount of humus needed for the average garden and the amount of organic debris available for the compost pile. Grass, sod, leaves, pine needles, weeds (if your compost pile is managed properly), and wood are generally available in sufficient amounts on your own property. Once you get a feel for composting, you'll quickly realize that there is a whole range of common but unconventional debris for your compost pile, like vacuum bag waste, hair, newspaper, and even human urine.

GRASS: The average residential landscape in the United States includes a lawn. The grass clippings that are generated by 30 or 40 mowings each season create an enormous volume of yard waste. Many people still collect their clippings. If your lawn has gone a long time between cuttings or your plan is to overseed, it's best to catch the clippings. In these cases, they are an excellent contribution to the compost pile.

Grass clippings are good for composting only if they are mixed with leaves or some other dry material, such as straw, hay, sawdust, or even Canadian sphagnum peat moss. Because they are almost entirely water, fresh grass clippings piled alone compact rapidly so there is no air in the pile. This causes an anaerobic (without oxygen) situation and the clippings will essentially putrefy, begin to smell, and turn slimy. Dried in the sun first or combined with dry brown materials, clippings decompose properly.

With the widespread availability of mulching lawnmowers, however, many homeowners now leave their clippings right on the lawn to decompose and provide nitrogen directly to grass plants. This is one of the best methods for improving the health of your lawn. The nitrogen in the clippings (see page 37 for nitrogen levels) goes directly back into the soil as the clippings rapidly break down on the soil surface. They add a bit of organic material directly to the soil, too, thanks to the earthworms that pull the clippings down into the soil to feed on them.

Even if you mulch your grass clippings into your lawn, you may find that your neighbors who still collect and bag their clippings are a good source. To guard against the inadvertent introduction of herbicides or other pesticide residues into the compost pile, forage clippings that were collected after a heavy rain. The rain will have washed contaminants, if any, from the blades.

SOD: Chunks of sod are ideal for composting. Not only do you get the nitrogen from the grass, but there is usually some topsoil around their roots that tends to be rich in nutrients. Along with the grass and soil, you will be adding some good organisms to your pile as well. The drawback with sod is that it requires a year or two to become fully decomposed if it's left as big strips. To compost it alone, dampen the pieces and stack them, grass side facing down, into a pile. Cover them with a tarp to keep out the light and they will become compost in about two years. An alternative to hasten sod's decomposition is chopping or shredding it into small pieces and mixing the pieces with the other materials in your regular pile.

LEAVES: The real composting windfall is leaves. Here is where homeowners with several large deciduous shade trees reap the rewards for all the effort put into raking leaves. While fallen leaves represent a large percentage of the total yard waste produced by the landscape every year, they are also the best way to ensure the landscape's health. Some homeowners shred them with a mulching mower or leaf shredder and use them immediately as mulch under their trees and shrubs. Used in this manner, the leaves decompose gradually in place and condition the soil. Even after all the mulching is done, there are usually lots of leaves left for the compost pile. Whole leaves decompose eventually, but they take up more space and decompose in twice the time of chopped leaves.

Any kind of leaves can be composted. Whether they're acidic or alkaline at the start of decomposition, the resulting compost will have an almost neutral pH (6.8 to 7.2). While pine needles, oak leaves, and coffee grounds are naturally acidic and make ideal mulch for acid-loving plants (blueberry, azalea, and rhododendron, for example) or as an additive to soil that tends to be alkaline, composting makes them essentially neutral in pH.

PINE NEEDLES: Pine needles, along with needles from trees like spruce, bald cypress, and fir, are "leaves" too. However, most needled trees and shrubs are evergreen, so their needles do not fall in large quan-

WHAT NOT TO COMPOST:

- Sawdust from pressure-treated lumber
- Chips or sawdust from allelopathic trees (black walnut, eucalyptus, red cedar, and others with aromatic oils)
- Meat or meat products like gravy, fats, and bones
- Dairy products, such as cheese, whole eggs, sour cream, or milk
- Used pet litter or pet feces
- Human feces
- Ashes from a coal stove, or charcoal ashes
- Diseased garden plants
- Grass clippings treated with pesticides or herbicides
- Invasive weeds (seeds can survive a passive pile)
- Poison ivy

tities over a short period of time. They age and fall throughout the year, often forming their own lovely mulch beneath the tree or shrub. They also make good carbon additions (brown material) to the compost pile. If you choose to compost them, bear in mind that they take a bit longer to decompose than ordinary leaves. They have a thick outer coating of a waxy substance called cutin, which is slow to break down. And like ordinary leaves, they will decompose faster if they're shredded before being put in the pile.

WEEDS: Invariably, there is a fair amount of fresh, nitrogen-rich plant debris (green material) generated in the typical home landscape over a growing season. If there is a vegetable garden, there are also lots of discarded plants from the first round of cool-weather vegetables, then warm-weather crops, and eventually more cool-weather vegetable plants. Because they are green, they contribute nitrogen (see page 37 for nitrogen levels) to fuel the decomposition process.

There is the same potential problem with fresh weeds and other green plant debris that you might have with grass. Unless they are mixed in with generous amounts of brown material, they are likely to become anaerobic and begin to smell. Avoid this by stirring them into your leaf pile with lots of brown material. The other consideration is that some weeds and vegetable plants, especially mature ones, become fibrous. Plants such as tomato vines, Canadian thistle, and water hyacinth will compost more quickly if they are cut up or shredded first.

COMPOSTING WEEDS

If freshly discarded plants have set seed, think twice about adding them to your pile. Only the active method of composting (see page 39) generates temperatures hot enough (140° to 160°F within the pile) to kill seeds. With the passive method, you risk spreading viable seeds back over the yard with your finished compost. (You know this has happened when you have tomato plants coming up everywhere.) If you plan to use the passive composting method, throw invasive weeds such as quack grass, wild morning glory, and buttercup in the trash.

WOODY MATERIALS: Materials such as wood chips, pinecones, bark, prunings, and cleared brush are considered woody—brown and fibrous. Because they are tough, they take a long time to decompose, even when they have been shredded or chopped. But they make excellent compost. Heavy-duty shredders will grind or shred sticks and limbs fine enough so they can be routinely incorporated into a regular compost pile. The resulting compost has a slightly coarser texture, but it will be fine for use in all situations.

Some experienced composters put woody materials in a separate pile so that they don't become a nuisance when other, finer materials have become compost. Some gardeners actually prefer to mix the sticks, pinecones, and other woody debris right in with the leaves, grass, and other fine materials. The belief is that their presence helps to aerate the pile. While they do keep air spaces open during the decomposition process, sticks have to be sifted or separated from the finished product because they are not fully decomposed.

COMPOSTING WOOD

There are a few trees and shrubs that are not suitable for composting. They produce chemicals or resins that adversely affect nearby plants. There is evidence that these chemicals are still active even when the wood has decomposed into compost and would have a harmful effect on growing plants if they were incorporated into the soil. Black walnut, red cedar, and eucalyptus are the most common. The best way to recycle the wood from these trees is to make wood chips for use on permanent paths or driveways where they are not in any contact with your plants.

MATERIALS FROM INSIDE THE HOUSE: The typical American kitchen is a wonderful source of organic material for the compost pile. More than 200 pounds of garbage per year is often fed down the disposal or thrown away. Most of this "garbage" is perfect for your compost pile and, eventually, your soil.

KITCHEN WASTE: Fruit and vegetable peelings, stale baked goods, used coffee grounds, paper towels, tea bags, overripe fruit, soggy paper, and eggshells can go into the compost pile. In fact, almost any organic material from the kitchen is suitable, except meat or meat derivatives. As a rule, don't put meat or dairy products such as bones, grease, gravy, cheese, whole eggs, sour cream, or milk into your pile. Treat the usable kitchen scraps as you would fresh weeds and plants, mixing them with large amounts of dry carbon material, such as chopped leaves, brush, or wood chips, to prevent odor problems.

There are some circumstances where meat and dairy products can be recycled through composting, but they're not appropriate for a regular compost pile. Products high in fat, like salad dressings, mayonnaise, and peanut butter, also require very high temperatures generated by an active

Simple compost piles are merely collections of yard debris left to decompose on their own.

pile to safely decompose. Otherwise, they may smell and attract unwanted pest wildlife.

PAPER: There are several alternatives for recycling the enormous amount of paper that often accumulates in the average American household. One way to keep it out of the regular waste stream and landfills is to participate in your community recycling program, if there is one.

The water-based inks used for newspapers make them safe for composting in the backyard. If you have a home office, your copy and computer paper will also compost nicely. It's best to shred the paper first. If you have access to an electric shredder, this is a simple operation. Newspapers and office paper will also go through a large general-purpose landscape shredder just fine, but don't try it on a windy day.

WOOD ASHES: Another organic material generated inside the house is wood ashes. The compost pile is one place to dispose of ashes from a woodstove or fireplace. Used sparingly, they are very useful to break down acidic materials like pine needles or oak leaves. Their presence in the pile adds alkalinity

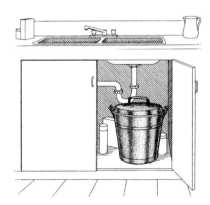

A sealed container under the sink is a convenient place to store nonmeat waste for the compost pile.

to offset the acidic leaves. Wood ashes do cause a loss of nitrogen in the final compost product, but it is negligible.

HUMAN WASTE: While it's common elsewhere in the world to recycle human feces into growing fields as fertilizer, this practice risks introducing certain human diseases into the food chain. Incorporating feces into backyard compost piles is not advisable for the same reason. Several cities in the United States—Philadelphia and Milwaukee among them—have municipal sludge composting operations that process sewage by composting it with wood chips many times. However, this is not something to try in a backyard compost pile.

If you have caught the recycling bug and are anxious to recycle human waste from your household, investigate toilets specifically designed to compost human waste. They are sometimes called "waterless toilets" and are designed to compost human feces.

Chipper/shredders are an excellent investment for the compost enthusiast, and debris fed through them will decompose rapidly in the compost pile.

Human urine, however, is a possible ingredient in a backyard compost pile. Assuming that you and your family are healthy, typical urine is essentially sterile and the transmission of disease is not a concern. Rich in nitrogen (see page 37 for nitrogen levels), urine accelerates the decomposition of carbon materials such as chopped leaves. It's particularly useful in the fall when there are leaves everywhere, but not much fresh nitrogen-rich yard or kitchen waste. Urine will not cause an odor when it's sprinkled on the pile at normal strength or diluted with water and mixed in a bit. Undiluted and simply poured on top of the pile, it sometimes leaves a telltale odor for a day or two.

MISCELLANEOUS MATERIALS: Once you realize that virtually anything organic can be composted, your outlook toward things that you normally discard in the trash will change. While these random things don't represent a significant source of organic material for your pile, they do contribute some of the essential carbon and nitrogen to the process. And at the very least, they are kept out of the municipal waste stream.

Some organic materials from the home that can be composted are: the contents of the vacuum cleaner bag, human hair, and dead houseplants. Nonsynthetic fabric, such as cotton sheets, towels, clean diapers, or wool garments, are also suitable for composting. Be certain that they do not have chemical finishes on them, and cut them up into fine pieces before adding them to the pile. Sawdust from the basement workshop is good as long as it is not from pressure-treated wood. The same is true of packaging materials made of wood.

MATERIALS FROM BEYOND THE BACKYARD: The majority of raw materials for your compost pile will be found in and around your own home. If you live in an area where there are lots of deciduous trees, you should have no trouble acquiring sufficient leaves to make plenty of compost for your garden beds. There will probably be extra to chop with the mulching mower and use as mulch on all your plants throughout the year.

There are lots of other sources of organic material if you are short on leaves or just want to compost on a grander scale than your residential landscape can support. Nearby farms are a great source of organic material. Animal manures are especially rich sources of nutrients for composting (see page 37 for nitrogen levels). Chicken manure is the richest in basic nutrients, but must always be composted before being spread on the garden. For backyard use, manures of any kind should be aged or dried, if possible. Your neighbors will appreciate it because dried manures do not smell as pungent as fresh manures. They are also richer in nutrients than fresh manure.

Farmers may also have what they call spoiled straw or hay, which is wet and therefore useless to the farmer. Another option is animal bedding, which is mixed with manure from the stables or barn. Plain straw is also excellent for composting because it helps aerate the pile and contributes carbon. Hay is good, too, except it's more likely to have weed seeds in it. If you manage your pile so that it reaches high temperatures (see page 39), the heat should kill the seeds. Occasionally, bales of straw are available at construction sites where contractors have used them to control erosion during the earth-moving phase. Once the job is finished, the bales are of no value to the contractor, and you may be able to get them free of charge.

Local landscape and nursery operations are another good source of raw materials for the compost pile. Many landscape contractors welcome a place to dump the wood chips produced by their chippers to avoid interrupting a job. This already-shredded woody material is ideal for your pile as long as the tree was not diseased or recently sprayed with chemical insecticides. (Always ask the contractor why the tree was cut down.) Make sure that it was not a red cedar or one that has an allelopathic (poisonous) effect on other plants (see page 18).

If you live in a coastal area, seaweed is a good organic material for the compost pile. It's rich in trace elements and micronutrients and has roughly the organic content of farm manure. Fresh and damp, seaweed promotes rapid decomposition of other organic materials when they're mixed together. Because it's salty from the ocean, rinse seaweed with a hose or expose it to rain briefly before putting it on your pile. (Don't soak it or you will wash off a lot of the surface nutrients.) Compost it immediately when green and fresh, or dry it first, then add it to the pile. When dried, it has a slightly higher level of some nutrients. The seashore is a good place to find fish waste as well. Because it is meat, however, take pains to mix it in thoroughly with leaves and other materials to avoid attracting critters to your pile.

BEWARE OF RESIDUE

When considering commercial by-products for your compost pile—particularly cotton industry by-products—beware of the possibility that pesticide or herbicide residues are present in them. Often their presence is negligible, or the heat from the decomposition process will break down these compounds into harmless natural components. But take this possibility into consideration before using these materials for your pile.

There are lots of commercial sources of organic materials, depending on where you live. Local restaurants and supermarkets throw out enormous amounts of nonmeat waste such as vegetable trimmings. Local businesses shred and discard bags of office paper. Nearby barber shops and hairdressing salons produce lots of human hair, which is very rich in nitrogen. Local factories often discard tons of plant by-products, such as rice hulls, cotton and wool waste, sugarcane waste, molasses residue, tanbark, hops residue, grape skins, and apple pomace.

SIMPLE COMPOSTING

Establishing a system to produce compost in your backyard needn't be complicated. After all, organic debris will decompose eventually with or without assistance. How much time and energy you devote to the process depends on what you want to gain. Once you begin producing compost, you'll quickly learn that your results will often be equal to your effort. There are no hard-and-fast rules—it's a matter of personal preference.

Composting systems can range from basic to elaborate. Some people just want to recycle yard debris to avoid putting it in the trash and, ultimately, a landfill. It's environmentally responsible and just incidentally good for their landscape. For these people, composting is a means to an end, a way to clean up the yard. The compost that results is a bonus. Most gardeners who approach composting in this manner are pretty relaxed about the process. Nature does most of the work with only minor assistance from time to time.

Skilled and avid gardeners usually see composting as essential to building healthy soil and having productive gardens. They tend to be impatient, hurrying decomposition to produce as much compost as possible every growing season. They often seek out raw materials beyond their own property. They turn their piles periodically to speed up the decomposing process and build compost piles for maximum efficiency. For the enthusiast, composting is an integral part of gardening.

When it comes to actually making compost, the main difference among gardeners is how often they intervene in the natural process. Relaxed gardeners are essentially bystanders. They take a passive approach and let Nature do its work. This approach is called simple composting. More avid gardeners take an active role in the process, which is called managed composting.

Most people fall somewhere between the two extremes. How deeply you become involved in composting will be a function of the time and effort you want to devote to it. The space and raw materials you have available also factor into your potential commitment to composting. Your composting system should suit your situation, and the right fit will evolve over time.

Making the Simple Compost Pile

A simple pile of organic materials allowed to decompose on its own is a good first foray into composting. This passive approach is very low maintenance. It requires little time and effort: collect the organic materials, dump them at the designated spot, and wait for them to become compost. The compost produced in this way is essentially the same as compost produced by the managed method.

What separates simple from managed composting is how the pile is prepared and monitored. A simple compost pile is basically a heap of discarded leaves, weeds, prunings, and grass clippings (if you're unable to mulch them into the lawn). This pile usually sits somewhere at the back of your property—indefinitely. Generally, it's viewed as a depository for yard debris. Over time the pile settles as the materials inside it gradually decompose. It grows again when you periodically add more raw materials to it. And all you have to do is dig into the base of the pile every so often and shovel out the finished compost. There are, however, some practices that make simple composting easier.

Woody materials like twigs, branches, old vines, and bark decompose so slowly, it's a good idea to cut them into smaller pieces with pruners or even a chipper machine. Your pile will no longer resemble a haphazard brush pile, and the woody pieces will break down more efficiently. Smaller pieces mix better with the other organic materials in your pile, thereby speeding the entire process. At their most basic level, simple piles are usually uncovered and unenclosed, so it's not a good idea to include kitchen scraps that may attract critters like skunks, rats, and dogs.

Without assistance, a simple pile won't produce much compost for a few years. Typically, simple piles are mostly carbon (brown) material, unevenly interspersed with small amounts of nitrogen (green) material. Air is usually scarce in the center of the pile, and moisture is rare. All these factors combine to slow the process of decomposition considerably.

Eventually, some finished humus becomes available at the bottom of the pile under the layers of organic material, which are at different stages of decomposition. Dig into the bottom of the pile once a year, or pull off the top layers of relatively raw material to get at the compost. Then reestablish the pile and continue to add to it as usual. Simple piles typically produce only a few bushels of finished compost each year, but they do recycle the organic materials on your property effectively.

ENCLOSING THE SIMPLE PILE: Enclosing your simple pile in some sort of bin doesn't involve much time and energy. It improves the look of the pile and aids the decomposition process measurably. Bins can be elaborate or simple, depending on your needs. If your intent is to let the pile decompose without intervention, bin size and shape are not important. The most efficient enclosures, however, range in size from 3' × 3' × 3' to 5' × 5' × 5'. Even on their own, piles this size decompose much quicker than those bigger or smaller.

More important than the size

SUGGESTED MATERIALS FOR SIMPLE PILE ENCLOSURES

Chicken wire
Hardware cloth
Stacked bricks, cement blocks, or
  stones
Shipping pallets
Sheets of lattice
Old fencing/snow fencing
Drainage tiles

is that the materials be piled loosely. Whether your pile accumulates over time or is built all at once, don't pack the raw materials in too tightly.

Organisms in simple piles don't get much air, so you don't want to retard decomposition by further compressing the pile.

A basic model is a three-sided, uncovered enclosure. The open side permits you to easily add to the pile, dig at the base, and recover finished compost. Simple piles also fare well in cylindrical wire-mesh cages or cinder-block enclosures—if they can be removed or opened with ease. A cover is optional because time is not of the essence in a simple pile. There is no need to maintain a hot temperature or protect it from the rain.

ENCOURAGING THE SIMPLE PILE: Because the simple pile produces compost slowly, you may become tempted to get more involved in the decomposition process. A modest effort can make the process dramatically more efficient. There are several techniques that speed decomposition but don't substantially increase the physical labor. To encourage a simple pile, make sure the four essentials—air, moisture, carbon, and nitrogen—are present.

ADDING AIR: Though they sit for months and even years, simple piles usually have only a small amount of air in them to support the organisms that aid in decomposition. If more air is fed into the center of the pile, the entire process speeds up. The trick is to create air access without spending the time and effort to mix or turn the pile. There are lots of alternatives for injecting air into a simple pile. Most involve either inserting vents into the pile or building a frame within the pile so that stacked raw materials don't get compressed when the pile grows.

One method involves placing two or three sturdy poles across a freestanding pile when it's halfway built and then again when it's three-quarters built. When the pile settles and compresses, the ends of the poles that protrude from the pile can be rolled or shaken to disturb the pile a bit, stimulating microbial activity.

Another alternative is to set one or more perforated PVC pipes (like plumbers use) vertically in the center of the compost area so they protrude from the top of the

Injecting air into a simple pile with pipes greatly speeds decomposition.

pile as it's built. This provides a permanent conduit for air into the center of the pile. Variations on this technique involve rolling up snow fencing and positioning it in the same way.

Raising the pile off the ground also admits air into it. The most effective way to do this is by building the pile on industrial shipping pal-

Building a simple pile on a shipping pallet allows air into the pile from the bottom and makes harvesting finished compost easier.

lets. If you combine this method with the vertical PVC pipe vent, the pile can yield finished compost in six to eight weeks.

REDUCING PARTICLE SIZE: Organisms responsible for decomposition work on the surfaces of organic materials in the pile. They can work faster and more efficiently if more surfaces are available to them. Taking the time to cut, chop, or shred organic materials prior to depositing them on the pile is one of the best methods to speed decomposition.

Since additions to a simple pile are usually haphazard, carbon and nitrogen materials tend to be in separate clumps throughout the pile. If the materials are shredded into uniform-size pieces and are able to mix a bit on their own, the decomposition will be more even throughout the pile without having to mix or turn it.

There are lots of ways to chop or shred materials for your pile. Sometimes all it takes is pruners or loppers to cut up sticks, twigs, and vines into 3" or 4" lengths. Leaves can be shredded easily as you mow the lawn. If you have a mulching mower with a bagging attachment, just mow the leaves where they fall and empty the bag on your pile. Shredder vacuums make it possible to pick up leaves and shred them as they flow into a bag on your shoulder. Nylon string trimmers (see page 61) also do a good job of shredding leaves. Simply put the leaves in a large trash can and use the string trimmer like a blender.

Lastly, when you are doing large-scale yard cleanup, it may be worthwhile to rent or borrow a shredder/chipper. Just run the debris through the machine and throw it on your pile.

ADDING DECOMPOSING ORGANISMS: Simple piles are rich environments for cool-temperature microorganisms to feed and reproduce in, decomposing materials in the process. The organic debris deposited in a compost pile already contains lots of these different kinds of bacteria. Most are in a dormant state, waiting until they have the air, moisture, carbon, and nitrogen to stimulate them into action.

One theory holds that the more organisms present, the faster decomposition occurs. If you're looking to speed things up in your simple pile, adding more organisms may help. Toss some shovelfuls of regular soil on the pile every so often as the materials accumulate, and you will introduce more organisms, which are happy to take advantage of newly available organic material. A population explosion is often the result. One handful of even mediocre soil with minimal humus content contains billions of microbes ready to do their job. In lieu of soil, you can recycle some of your finished compost back into the pile and accomplish the same thing.

ADDING COMMERCIAL BIOACTIVATOR PRODUCTS: If you frequent garden centers or receive garden mail-order catalogs, you're probably aware of the numerous compost-accelerating products on the market. Sometimes called activators or catalysts, they are usually combinations of microbial organisms, enzymes, and other natural components involved in the complex decomposition process. They are commonly packaged in dry form to be sprinkled on the pile every so often as you add deposits of organic yard waste. Moisture on the surfaces of the debris activates the organisms, and they quickly go to work.

ADDING WORMS: Because they don't heat up, simple compost piles normally attract lots of invertebrate decomposers, such as millipedes, sowbugs, and earthworms. These critters migrate throughout the pile to help decompose the organic materials. Within a week or two in warm weather, a newly built pile will become home to lots of these helpers. However, if your local supply is sparse, you may want to add more earthworms. One way is to collect earthworms from the garden and transfer them into the pile. Bait worms for fishing also adjust happily to the pile.

Special worms are raised specifically for composting because they are very efficient at breaking down organic material. Called "red wigglers" or red composting worms, they are available through mail order for about $28 for 2 lbs. They are not, however, able to survive in regular soil, so you need to be sure that they are transferred to fresh organic materials when the decomposition of their current pile is nearly completed. They

---

TROUBLESHOOTING SIMPLE COMPOST PILES

PROBLEM	SOLUTION
Bad odor	Avoid too much nitrogen-rich material; cover with carbon (brown) material
Matted leaves	Cut or shred large materials before adding to pile
Lumpy, sticks protrude	Cut or shred large materials before adding to pile
Weed sprouts	Avoid putting weeds that have set seed on pile
Critters	Use only woody materials; avoid using garbage

For more on pile problems, see SOLVING COMPOST PROBLEMS (pages 91–102).

---

will die of starvation otherwise. These are the same worms sold with worm composting kits for processing garbage (see page 100).

ADDING NITROGEN: The materials in the average simple pile are overwhelmingly carbon. At any given time the amount of leaves, twigs, bark, and other woody debris is far greater than the green weeds and kitchen scraps that provide nitrogen. Decomposition is often terribly slow because there is little nitrogen to spur the activity of organisms. A simple way to remedy the imbalance somewhat is to run your kitchen peelings through the blender and liquefy them with some water so that they can be poured onto the pile. In liquid form, they penetrate the simple pile easily, promoting more uniform mixing of carbon and nitrogen and, thus, faster decomposition.

Other Simple Composting Methods

If you have only a small amount of organic waste or a very small property with limited space for composting, there are other simple ways to compost. "Sheet" composting is a system that involves spreading raw organic materials directly in the garden in relatively thin layers instead of in a pile. Put a 2" or 3" layer of chopped leaves directly on the soil in your planting bed, and then, if available, add a layer of grass clippings on top. You can till or mix this in as you plant or leave it over the winter. The earthworms and other microbes in the soil will break it down over time.

Some gardeners with limited space dig holes in their beds with shovels or posthole diggers and fill them with garbage and finely cut-up yard debris. Covered with soil, these mini-piles gradually decompose and fertilize the garden without any further effort by the gardener. Try this in areas that are not being planted immediately.

Managed Composting

While simple composting is a reasonably efficient way to recycle organic debris, it's not an ideal method for producing large amounts of compost. Simple piles decompose at their own pace and produce compost in small amounts, which is adequate for incidental soil improvement only. In order to impact your soil significantly, larger amounts of compost are necessary—and this is best achieved through a managed composting system.

You may find that it's worth the increased time and effort to take an active role in the composting process and reap greater rewards. If you're prepared to manage the decomposition process in your pile—intervening in a variety of ways to fine-tune its efficiency—you'll have much more compost to improve your soil.

The main difference between the decomposition process in a simple pile and in a managed pile is the temperature of the environment. In a managed pile you manipulate the materials so that the center of the pile heats up enough to stimulate the activity of highly efficient thermophilic organisms (see page 8). In short, managing a compost operation involves helping the pile to "cook." Your efforts will revolve around keeping the organisms active and sustaining the high internal temperature as long as possible. One of the primary ways to do this is by periodically infusing the piled materials with air, thereby supporting the aerobic (air-breathing) organisms.

As the compost pile decays, these organisms consume the available air at its core; as the amount of air diminishes, so does the rate of decomposition and the temperature. When you add air to the pile by turning or mixing when the temperature drops, it stimulates the organisms to renewed activity. Aeration is fundamental to managed compost piles. Combined with other techniques, it's possible to make the decomposition process so efficient that you can harvest a batch of compost in just a few weeks.

THE PROS AND CONS OF MANAGED COMPOSTING

Before diving headlong into undertaking a managed compost pile, it's important to consider the advantages and disadvantages of this approach over the simple pile. The main disadvantage is obvious at the outset: to be involved in the decomposing process at all requires a lot more time and energy. You must collect and process more materials, and turn the pile. Managed piles require more space because you're likely to have several—one or two actively cooking, with others acting as holding piles for unprocessed organic materials. You will also need some equipment, which is a financial investment.

If your goal is to produce compost in sufficient quantities to improve the soil over your entire yard, however, the advantages of a managed compost pile are significant. The result will be more compost much sooner.

BUILDING THE MANAGED COMPOST PILE

If you intend to manage your composting operation, you will need to build your pile with more care and thus ensure faster decomposition. There are no strict rules, but randomly tossing organic debris in a heap will not result in very efficient compost production.

Many gardeners build their piles gradually with what is readily available at the time. Most of the year, however, there is simply not enough organic yard debris to build a full-size pile all at once. As a result, the pile grows incrementally from periodic additions. Since leaves are the most abundant organic material in many backyards, they make up the bulk of

Serial bins—identical bins arranged in a row— make managed composting easier.

the pile at any given time. These piles are usually less than optimum size most of the time and are essentially simple piles with prospects. While piles that just "happen" will decompose (especially if you follow the management steps described below), this method is not as efficient as it could be.

If possible, it's best to "create" a pile all at once. Ideally, you want to build your pile to an optimum size in one session from materials you have saved and stored in a heap or in trash bags until you have them in sufficient quantities. The storage requires more space (see pages 45–47), but you can have both carbon and nitrogen materials ready at the same time. The materials should also be available in enough volume to achieve the critical mass for efficient decomposition—about 3' × 3' × 3' or 4' × 4' × 4'.

Contrary to what some experts say, it's not necessary to build a pile in alternating layers of green and brown materials. Nor it is necessary to include other ingredients. While adding layers of fertilizer, topsoil, lime, or activator does no harm, it's an unnecessary effort and expense. There are lots of organisms in the pile already, and they have plenty to eat. If they get the air and moisture they need, they will see to it that even the most acidic materials end up about neutral in pH.

What does help is to have the materials in small pieces so that they offer lots of surface area. Small pieces break down at roughly the same rate, so they promote uniform decomposition. And be sure to construct the pile so it's not compacted. Lots of air spaces will fuel the activity of the decomposing organisms.

Remember, decomposition requires carbon, nitrogen, air, and, finally, moisture. If you have a pile that accumulates over time (rather than one that is constructed all at once), leaving it open to light rain periodically will moisten the ingredients sufficiently until they are covered by more materials. However, you'll want to cover the pile to avoid a soaking rain, which will cool the temperature building in the pile's core.

If you construct your pile all at once, the best way to assure moisture throughout the pile is to use damp materials. If it has not rained recently, wet down your storage pile or the contents of the trash bags with a hose before adding the materials to the pile. They should be moist, but not soggy. Once the pile is built, cover it to keep out rain. In fact, you may want to enclose the whole pile.

A pile that incorporates the essential ingredients and is the correct size will start cooking almost immediately. After a day or two, if you stick your hand toward the center, you will be able to feel the heat. The trick is to keep it cooking until all of the raw materials are reduced to humus. In the natural order of things, the organisms in the core of the pile will use up the available air in a matter of days, and their activity will gradually cease. So it's up to you to keep things going by mixing the pile.

TURNING THE PILE: The single most important thing you can do to promote efficient decomposition of raw materials is to turn the pile. This reenergizes the decomposing organisms by providing them with new air as well as new materials to work on.

Typically, a "cooking" compost pile settles as the materials at its core decompose. Within a week or two it may reduce in size by as much as 30% from this activity as well as from basic gravity. The settling materials compress the air out of the pile, and it becomes very dense. Turning the pile fluffs it up as it aerates and renews the decomposing activity.

There are lots of techniques for turning the pile. If space is limited, one method is to simply stir the piled materials in place. Try to mix the outside, or relatively unprocessed organic particles, in toward the pile's interior. At the same time, bring the recently cooked compost out toward the cooler edges of the pile.

Compost-aerating tools purportedly make this task easier, but they're not necessary. The typical aerating tool is a pole about 4' long with a pointed tip. After the pole is inserted deep into the core of the pile and then withdrawn a bit, flanges flip out to agitate the material. This tool injects some air into the center of the pile but is not as effective as restacking it. Aerating tools are also difficult to use if the pile has settled and become so compressed that there's not much space to insert the tool. A tined composting or manure fork is definitely the best tool for turning and aerating a pile that has settled.

Mixing a pile in place requires a lot of physical effort and doesn't actually mix the materials very well. Some compost enthusiasts turn their piles by digging the materials out of the existing bin or pile, putting them aside, and then returning them to the original empty space or bin. While this method certainly does the job, it actually does it twice, and the physical energy needed to move the volume of organic material two times is substantial.

ORGANISM ACCESS

One of the benefits of turning a compost pile—besides adding lots of oxygen for the microbial life in the pile—is mixing the different kinds of micro- and macroorganisms throughout the material. Make sure that the material on the outside of the pile moves to the inside, so each type of organism has access to all of the pile over time. That is why a pile that has been turned once or twice yields much more uniformly textured compost.

The most common way to turn the compost pile is by digging out the material from the existing pile and restacking it in a new spot right next to the old one. The simple act of taking forkfuls of organic material and dumping them at a new spot mixes the materials and infuses the pile with air. The new pile becomes the active pile, the old spot becomes storage space, and you have handled the material just once.

If you enclose your pile, the design of the enclosure is important. It helps tremendously if it opens in front so you can dig out its contents. A good alternative bin design dismantles easily or can be simply lifted from around the pile so you can work its contents. Serial bins—two or three enclosures in a row that provide front and top access—make this restacking or turning technique easier and neater. You can even keep two piles cooking at varying stages of decomposition and easily turn them in rotation.

Stackable composters work by inverting the three tiers of the stack, thereby aerating the pile and allowing access to finished compost.

There are no strict rules for turning the pile. You may decide to turn it more than once. For example, a week or two after the first turning, when it begins to cool down, is a good time for a second turning. If the materials are not yet reduced to humus, an additional aeration will accelerate the process. When you turn the pile a second time, you'll find that most of the organic material has become evenly dark brown and moist. The exception is the 4" to 6" layer of gray powdery material just beneath the thin outside crust of unprocessed debris. This is a zone where cool-temperature fungi are particularly active.

As you dig into the pile, the material at the very center may still be hot enough to produce steam when the cool ambient air reaches it. If all the materials have been thoroughly mixed by turning the pile once or twice, the pile will eventually cool for good. This occurs because all of the organisms have converted the materials into humus and there is nothing more

COMMON MATERIALS FOR COMPOSTING

HIGH-NITROGEN MATERIALS These items should not be composted by themselves; they need some carbon materials to balance the high nitrogen levels.

MATERIAL	SOURCE OF	C/N RATIO	% NITROGEN
Alfalfa	N	13–20 to 1	2.5–3
Bone meal	N	3 to 1	L–2
Coffee grounds	N	20 to 1	2
Fish scraps	N	5 to 1	2–8
Grass clippings	N	12–25 to 1	1–2
Kitchen garbage, raw	N	12–25 to 1	2
Manure, chicken	N	7–10 to 1	3.2
Manure, cow	N	18 to 1	1.7
Manure, horse	N	25 to 1	2.3
Urine, human	N	8 to 1	15–18

MATERIALS WITH BOTH CARBON AND NITROGEN These materials will decompose effectively if mixed with some other high-carbon and high-nitrogen materials.

MATERIAL	SOURCE OF	C/N RATIO	% NITROGEN
Leaves	C/N	30–80 to 1	L–1
Manure, rotted	C/N	20 to 1	1–5
Seaweed, washed	C/N	19 to 1	1–2
Weeds, fresh	C/N	18 to 1	L–2

HIGH-CARBON MATERIALS These materials will decompose effectively if mixed with some high-nitrogen materials.

MATERIAL	SOURCE OF	C/N RATIO	% NITROGEN
Hay, timothy	C	58 to 1	.85
Paper	C	150–200 to 1	–
Newspaper, shredded	C	800 to 1	.05
Sawdust, aged	C	208 to 1	.25
Sawdust, fresh	C	500 to 1	1
Straw, wheat	C	128 to 1	.3
Straw, oat	C	80 to 1	1.05
Wood chips	C	700 to 1	L

for them to do. It's now time for you to harvest the compost and start a fresh pile.

FINE-TUNING THE CARBON/NITROGEN (C/N) RATIO: A pile of virtually nothing but carbon materials and the requisite air and moisture will eventually decompose. However, adding even relatively few nitrogen (green) materials galvanizes the process. And it doesn't take much nitrogen to speed up decomposition dramatically.

If you are managing your pile intensely, you may want to pay attention to how much nitrogen is present relative to the volume of carbon materials. These proportions are commonly referred to as the carbon/nitrogen (C/N) ratio. Typically, a ratio of about 30 to 1 (carbon to nitrogen materials) is adequate, and a pile will heat up to desired temperatures at that rate.

If you want your pile to heat up faster or to get hotter, then add more nitrogen materials. A ratio of 20 to 1—for instance, 20 bags of chopped leaves to 1 bag of chopped fresh weeds or grass clippings—will get things moving more efficiently. You can reduce the ratio to as low as 5 to 1, but any lower than that is not recommended or the pile will certainly begin to putrefy.

The trick is to avoid using more nitrogen than is needed to fuel the decomposition process. Green materials are usually less

MANAGING TEMPERATURE

For the truly obsessed there is something to learn from commercial composting operations. To get high-quality compost in the shortest possible time, commercial gardeners have discovered that decomposition occurs in the pile most efficiently when the internal temperatures range consistently from 104° to 131°F. Normally, since backyard gardeners only turn their piles occasionally, pile temperatures spike to 150°F and then naturally dip to a much cooler 100°F before the pile is turned again. This is an inevitable consequence of adding air, which tends to cool things a bit temporarily. The experience of commercial producers suggests that it's more efficient to turn the pile sooner— when your thermometer shows the pile has reached only 131°F. This more frequent intervention sustains optimum temperature longer and yields finished compost in about three weeks.

abundant, but it's better to use as much as you can to promote optimum temperatures. Of course, if you have too much nitrogen in a pile, it destroys the normal decomposition process, compressing the pile into an anaerobic heap that rapidly putrefies. An unpleasant smell signals too much nitrogen.

DOING IT ALL

The ultimate management of the composting process involves taking all of the previously mentioned steps. While most gardeners are content to intervene occasionally by turning the pile or adding more nitrogen materials if a pile doesn't heat up fast enough, there are a few enthusiastic gardeners who delight in participating fully in the process. They usually want as much compost as possible in a short period of time, and they're willing to acquire and process as much organic raw materials as needed. And they take all of the management steps to make the process as efficient as possible.

Composting is a highly individual activity. If you find yourself eager to go the whole way, plan to develop a system and acquire the equipment to manage the decomposition process from beginning to end.

Begin by storing off-season materials until you have sufficient quantities to build a 4' × 4' × 4' pile in the spring in some sort of bin that

KILLING WEED SEEDS AND DISEASE PATHOGENS

Turning a compost pile keeps it cooking and produces compost faster. The other important reason to turn the pile is to ensure that any weed seeds or disease pathogens that accompanied your raw organic materials into the pile are also killed.

For this to happen, internal pile temperatures should reach at least 130°F for a day or two. To sustain temperatures that high, it's important to have sufficient nitrogen (N) in the pile to fuel the decomposition activity. If a pile is almost all carbon (C), such as a pile of chopped leaves with just a small amount of fresh weeds (90 to 1), then it will not heat up enough to kill weed seeds and disease pathogens.

While most disease pathogens will die after being in a temperature of about 130°F for 10 to 15 minutes, some weed seeds require temperatures between 140° and 150°F to kill them completely. A good C/N ratio to achieve these temperatures is 20 to 1, and up to 40 to 1.

A full-scale managed composting operation includes three serial bins, a storage area, as well as a range of equipment for shredding and turning the compost.

can be covered. For maximum efficiency, shred the materials and mix them to reach a C/N ratio of about 30 to 1. If you want to use a commercial compost bioactivator product, this is the time to add it.

Using a compost thermometer, monitor the temperature at the center of the pile. When it reaches between 130° and 150°F (go with the lower temperature if you do not need to worry about weed seeds or disease pathogens), turn the pile. By adding a bit more nitrogen material, you can increase the heat.

At this stage, you may also want to run the whole pile through the shredder again to further reduce particle size and thoroughly mix the particles from various depths of the pile, which are at different stages of decomposition. (Earthworms will probably migrate to your pile after you build it initially, and they will not survive shredding.)

If you participate to this extent in the decomposition process, you will have bushels and bushels of finished compost within weeks. And if you have enough raw materials, space, and energy, you can manage several piles simultaneously to double and triple your production.

COMPOSTING SITES

The location of your compost pile should be a prime consideration in your composting scheme. It should be situated in an area that's both convenient and unobtrusive. While these two needs are often at cross-purposes, it's possible to find a satisfactory spot in most backyards. In many cases, the size of your yard will be a deciding factor. And a larger yard does not always mean greater convenience.

The problem of location is usually easier to solve in smaller yards, where space is limited. There are fewer site possibilities, and most options are likely to be easily accessible. Creative use of landscape plants and decorative features can effectively screen your pile from view, even if it's relatively close to the back door or the garden. Another possibility for small yards is to persuade your neighbor to share the pile. Locating it on the boundary of adjacent properties makes it convenient to both parties and leaves more backyard living space for each family.

Much of your decision depends on whether you plan to maintain a simple pile or expect to get into managed composting. If you're not sure, choose a site for a simple pile that can be expanded in case you decide to upgrade your operation. Another logical option for locating a pile is near an established work area. Every yard has one or more utility areas for trash cans, toolsheds, garden carts, and unused flowerpots. Regardless of the size and complexity of your compost operation, it should be considered part of the utility area and located there.

GENERAL SPECIFICATIONS

B e sure to locate compost piles and bins on soil—not on a paved surface. This way, the pile can drain into the soil below. Earthworms and microbes that live in soil can migrate into the pile and contribute to its decomposition. Also, composting sites should be essentially level. If level ground is at a premium, site the actual compost pile there and store raw materials elsewhere close by, on uneven or sloping ground.

A primary consideration when planning a compost site is to allow enough space for you to work, as well as room for cart and wheelbarrow access.

When designating space for your composting operation, don't forget that you will be working in the area. You'll need access for a cart or wheelbarrow and some elbow room for moving around the pile as you build it. While there's no need to formally fence the area, it should be protected from access and the view of passersby, especially neighborhood children. Factoring in space for plantings or screens of some sort around the perimeter of the area is a good idea.

Locating a pile in sun or shade doesn't significantly affect the decomposition process. The heat of any pile is always more a function of its contents than of its light exposure. However, hot sun may dry outer

PLANTS TO SCREEN A COMPOSTING SITE

SHRUBS

Rhododendron
(*Rhododendron* spp.)
Viburnum (*Viburnum* spp.)
Forsythia (*Forsythia* spp.)
Privet (*Ligustrum* spp.)
Spirea (*Spirea* spp.)
Barberry (*Berberis* spp.)
Cotoneaster (*Cotoneaster* spp.)
Japanese Holly (*Ilex crenata*)
Azalea (*Rhododendron* spp.)

PERENNIALS

Sunflower (*Helianthus* spp.)
Joe Pye Weed
(*Eupatorium maculatum*)

Macleaya (*Macleaya* spp.)
Ostrich fern
(*Matteuccia struthiopteris*)

VINES

Honeysuckle (*Lonicera* spp.)
Lablab (*Lablab* spp.)
Clematis (*Clematis* spp.)
Kiwi (*Actinidia deliciosa*)
Morning Glory (*Ipomoea alba*)
Silver Lace (*Polygonum aubertii*)
Sweet Pea (*Lathyrus odoratus*)
Trailing Nasturtium
(*Tropaeolum majus*)
Virginia Creeper
(*Parthenocissus quinquefolia*)

portions of the pile, especially if it's not enclosed in a bin of some sort. This occurrence is more of a concern in hot, arid regions of the country, where dehydration is a problem. Elsewhere, most homeowners prefer to save the sunny areas for prime planting sites. If the only appropriate spot in your yard is sunny, however, don't fret.

Some shade can be a real advantage in a composting area. If the site receives shade at least part of the day, it's easier on the person who works there in the summer heat. If the tree that gives the shade is deciduous, you will have the best of both worlds. It will shade the pile in summer, and when the leaves fall in autumn, it will allow sun on the pile to sustain its temperature a bit longer into winter.

While shade from nearby trees is a blessing during episodes of intense heat, the proximity of trees to the compost pile can be problematic. Tree roots may begin to grow toward the surface of the soil where rich humus is developing at the bottom of the pile. They do this partly in search of nutrients; but deeply buried feeder roots, which typically prefer to be in the top 12" of soil, migrate toward the soil surface in search of air.

The roots of certain trees are more aggressive than others in infiltrating compost piles. Ailanthus, alder, black locust, eucalyptus, redwood, and willow are among the worst offenders. You can prevent the migration of roots into your pile if you move it sporadically. This should also be done with the location of your storage pile; as you harvest one and start another, try to vary the placement each time. Moving your bin slightly when you turn your active pile also discourages persistent tree roots.

Avoid situating your pile against or near a building, wall, or fence. At the very least, these positions limit air circulation around all sides of the pile. And if the wall is wood, the presence of decomposing organisms in the adjacent pile will begin to promote decay of the wall, too. The constant weight and moisture of the pile will mar the surface—even over a short period of time.

Positioning your pile downwind from your house and the neighbors is another smart precaution. A compost pile with lots of carbon materials and relatively few nitrogen materials rarely smells. From time to time, however, the C/N ratio may get a little skewed, especially in a simple pile that grows from a rarely mixed supply of raw organic materials. If a load of fresh weeds is thrown on top of a standing pile, for example, they will decay anaerobically and develop an odor until you mix in some carbon materials.

Exposure to strong wind is not necessarily an advantage to your compost pile. Whatever measure of aeration is achieved by good air circulation from a windy site is offset by the tendency for the pile to dry out. Since you will be stirring up enough dust and debris when you turn your pile, wind is generally unwelcome.

LOCATING A SIMPLE PILE: The size of a simple pile is usually related to the size of your yard. Because it's essentially a depository for the organic material from your yard, its size is rarely out of scale with your property. When you first start a simple pile, however, estimating its eventual size can seem difficult.

A small yard does not generate as many leaves, twigs, clippings, and weeds as a large one does. Because a simple pile gradually settles as the materials at its base decompose, its dimensions are relatively constant from year to year. If you keep this fact in mind, it will be easier to estimate the amount of space you'll need for your composting area. Be sure to add 6' to 8' on two sides in addition to whatever area you estimate for your pile. This allows space for a wheelbarrow or garden cart, plus room to wield a long-handled composting fork.

Simple piles have some particular location problems because they are essentially stationary. Unlike managed piles, which are more easily moved because of their size, simple piles may occupy the same spot for years. Invasive tree roots represent the most common problem. If trees are in close proximity to your pile, it's a good idea to build it on a base to separate it from the soil. You can put the pile on a concrete pad, on

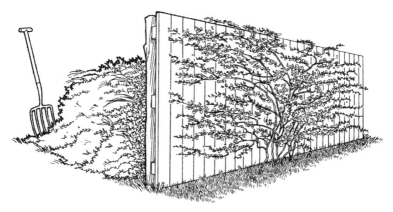

As long as your pile doesn't rest directly against it, a wooden fence can act as an excellent screen for a composting system.

sheets of scrap metal, or in a bin with a wood or plastic bottom. A vented base to let in some air—found on a commercial wooden pallet, cinder blocks, or a commercial bin—is probably the best option. Banking the area slightly to slope back prevents puddling and is a good idea in wet climates.

LOCATING A MANAGED SYSTEM: If your goal is to produce significant amounts of compost rather than to simply recycle yard waste, you'll need more room for your composting operation. To build a pile that will cook efficiently, you should have a supply of both green (nitrogen) and brown (carbon) materials sufficient to build one or more piles that are roughly 3' × 3' × 3' to 5' × 5' × 5'. Since each material is in abundance at different times of the year, some area must be allotted to

A grouping of low bushes—especially evergreen varieties—is particularly effective for screening a compost pile, as well as for discouraging children from playing around it.

store these materials. Typically, autumn leaves are stored either loose or in bags to use in spring when fresh weeds and clippings are available. If you expect to import raw organic materials from outside sources, allocate enough space to accommodate windfalls of straw, manure, wood chips, and so on.

Because managed piles are turned one or more times, plan extra space for this process. Factor in at least 6' to 8' of leeway around two or three sides of the pile for you to work in as you turn the pile or harvest finished compost. An adjacent area for turning your pile or removing and refilling bins is useful. An alternative to this is multiple bins. Both options require the same amount of space.

Allow space at the composting site for equipment as well. In addition to your composting fork, garden cart, various pails, and containers, you may eventually acquire a shredder or chipper. These are available in a range of sizes, and all require a significant amount of space for safe operation. Not only will you need to consider allocating space in your compost area for storage of the machine, but a sizable area is also necessary for the actual shredding and chopping done in preparation for building your compost pile. Often, this means assembling two piles: one that is about to be shredded and one that accumulates after it has been shredded. Because these machines are often high-powered, they should be considered dangerous. Working in tight quarters can lead to mishaps with these machines and is not recommended.

If you can't use finished compost right away, it's important to store it in trash cans, a separate bin, or even just as a pile. Be sure to cover it because rain will leach out its water-soluble nutrients. You may choose to store your finished compost near the planting areas, but if you plan for it to remain in the composting area, allow space for it.

SCREENING THE COMPOSTING AREA

Regardless of the size of your composting area, it's a good idea to screen it from view for both aesthetic and safety reasons. The screen can be something simple, like a fence made of landscape timbers. Another possibility is to extend a distinctive hardscape feature of your yard, such as a stone wall, lattice screen, or decorative fencing.

Using plants—alone or in combination with a wall or fence—to screen the compost area is also effective. A dense row of evergreens, such as arborvitae, azalea, holly, or yew, hides the compost area nicely and provides a backdrop for ornamental plants in the yard. Plants with prickly leaves or stems, such as barberry, holly, and pyracantha, are particularly effective at discouraging visits by adventurous children (just be sure the plants don't encroach on your work area).

Vines are useful, too, particularly fast-growing annual vines that can be easily persuaded to crawl over an open simple pile or storage heap and obscure it from view. Moonflower, morning glory, nasturtium, and sweet pea can transform an eyesore into a hill of colorful flowers. If the light is sufficient, train perennial vines such as clematis, honeysuckle, ivy, and Virginia creeper onto a fence or wall around the area to add ornamental interest.

A more elaborate alternative is to espalier a row of apple, fig, or pear trees on a fence to form the screen. Planted very closely, their foliage creates a solid green wall during the growing season. If completely screening the area is not feasible, strategically placed rhododendrons and other flowering shrubs that can handle the partial shade at your composting site make it more attractive. Resist the temptation to put pots or tubs of colorful annuals in the exposed area because they will simply draw attention to the pile.

The composting area of your yard is a utility area and has the same liabilities that any such area has. The main concern is that the site be an adequate size and conveniently located. Anything that you can do to disguise the fact that it's there is desirable.

Choosing *a* Compost Bin

Enclosing your compost pile in some sort of container is desirable whether you have a simple pile periodically mined for finished compost or a managed pile that you turn frequently. The main advantage is appearance. On a farm, compost piles can be easily hidden behind the barn or located in a remote area. However, typical backyard piles are often unavoidably visible, particularly in winter when trees and shrubs that might otherwise screen them from view are leafless. And organic materials being stored for eventual use in a managed pile can be unsightly unless you have several bins, cages, or enclosures to contain them.

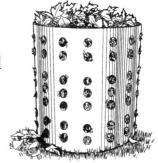

Another significant advantage to a compost bin is shelter from the elements. It's far easier to protect a pile from downpouring rain if you have a structure around it. While exposure to the elements is not a major concern with a simple pile, a managed one is designed to generate high temperatures at its core. Soaking rains reduce internal heat and the time it's sustained, thus slowing down the decomposition process. Excessive soaking will also mat nitrogen materials and precipitate an anaerobic and smelly pile.

A bin or enclosure will also protect your pile from visitors—both children and critters. Simple piles in particular attract attention from wildlife in search of food and nesting sites in suburban neighborhoods.

Lastly, a box or bin that encloses your pile or accumulated materials saves space. It controls the spread of the pile, confining it to the dimensions of the bin, and it restricts the volume of material to a size appropriate for limited space.

CRITERIA FOR A COMPOST BIN

When you decide to construct a bin or enclosure system, there are four basic issues to consider: design, size, price, and materials. It's important that your choices be flexible because your requirements may change over time. You may decide to switch from a simple to a managed system or to add another pile to the operation. You will undoubtedly develop preferences in design and probably change your system at least once. Fortunately, bins are relatively inexpensive, especially if you build one from recycled materials.

DESIGN: The design of your bin or enclosure should reflect the type of pile you want. In all cases, however, it should have slats or holes in the sides to encourage air circulation around the pile. Air access from the bottom of the pile is even more beneficial. While commercial bins rarely include a special base, it's easy to create one from a discarded wooden pallet or special mats offered for this purpose by some mail-order companies (see page 54).

Eventually, you'll need to get at the pile to harvest finished compost from the bottom. The best bins or enclosures feature convenient removable sides or a design that allows the entire bin to be lifted up and off the pile. A bin of stacked cinder blocks that can be dismantled on one side or a wire cage that can be unfastened on one side or lifted off the entire pile are examples of practical, yet simple designs. Whatever the construction material, the sides should be substantial enough to support a cover made from marine plywood, boards, or a simple tarp.

Managed piles require containers with a slightly more elaborate design. Because you'll be actively involved in the composting process, convenient access to the pile is crucial. A bin should have removable panels or sides sturdy enough to support the pile without warping or bowing. Like an enclosed simple pile, it should also include a cover to keep off the rain and snow. A bin with sides or layers that can be added incrementally as the pile grows is also a great convenience. The pile is supported, but you don't have to strain your back lifting materials up as high as the height of the box.

SIZE: The size of a bin or enclosure for a simple pile is not as critical to the decomposition process as it is with a managed pile. Storage heaps of raw materials intended for a managed pile tend to be large and irregularly shaped. The main concern with them (and with simple piles) is to make them less obtrusive, to enclose and shelter them from the elements, and to keep them from getting unmanageably tall.

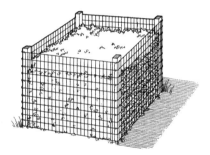

In contrast, the size of actively managed piles expected to develop high internal temperatures is more critical. Because they are usually built all at once, their size is easier to control. A pile's volume should be easily enclosed by a box or bin that resembles a cube whose height, width, and depth are some-

A simple wire mesh enclosure is an ideal storage bin for organic materials.

where between 3' and 5'. If you have more materials available, then plan for a second container to store them or build a second pile. Many commercial bins are slightly smaller than 3' × 3' × 3', but they are acceptable alternatives.

PRICE: Price is usually not an obstacle when selecting a good compost bin. You can fashion a homemade version from discarded materials for under $10. Bins for sale at garden centers, hardware stores, home centers, and mail-order outlets typically range in price from $40 up to $160. Price is a function of their materials, design, and size. And some models have expansion units that add onto the original bin, doubling its size. The additions are slightly less expensive than the basic bin unit.

The least expensive bins and boxes are usually made of bare wire or slats of waste lumber. The more expensive bins tend to be made of molded resin or plastic materials and feature air vents, lids, and often special liners to improve their efficiency.

MATERIALS: Homemade bins and boxes for compost piles provide a wonderful opportunity to recycle all kinds of materials: cinder blocks, various wire mesh and snow fencing, wooden shipping pallets, logs, or scrap lumber. If you're inclined to buy materials specifically for this purpose, some type of milled lumber is probably the least expensive. Slightly more expensive but very attractive are panels of prefabricated lattice available at home and garden centers. Plastic "lumber" fabricated from recycled mixed plastics is ideal for constructing compost bins and can last indefinitely.

Used for storage or as an active compost pile, lattice slats make excellent compost bins.

A more fragile substance, like wood, leaves you with unavoidable trade-offs. You can expect wood to decompose over time because it's in contact with air, moisture, nitrogen, and hoards of microorganisms. The least expensive wood is untreated pine, but it has the shortest life span as a compost bin. Other untreated lumber, such as redwood, cedar, and cypress, are naturally decay-resistant but considerably more expensive. Typically, they last eight to ten years under the conditions in and around the composting area. If you are a strict organic gardener, this is the best choice of wood for you.

Ultimately, pressure-treated lumber certified for outdoor use—specifically for use in contact with soil—can be expected to last 20 years or more and is moderately priced. There are justifiable concerns about using chemically treated materials in such close proximity to compost that may be added to soil where food crops grow. But the accumulated evidence of years of research suggests that there's no serious long-term problem with most treated products.

However, it doesn't hurt to take precautions to prevent possible leaching of chemicals into the compost materials. Allow the lumber to weather for several months prior to constructing the bin. This way, the residual gases from the chemical compounds have time to vaporize. Microbial activity in the compost pile has also been found to break down numerous residues on wood surfaces into harmless components. The exception to this is creosote, the type of preservative used on railroad ties and telephone poles, which is sometimes found in certain landscaping timbers. Avoid using creosote-preserved wood around soil intended for raising plants.

MAKING YOUR OWN BIN

If you have the inclination, time, and energy, constructing your own bin has several obvious advantages. The bin can be made a full 5' × 5' × 5', which takes advantage of the critical mass needed for the very highest core temperatures in a managed pile. (This size is also ideal for a simple pile or for storage because it holds enormous amounts.) Most commercially manufactured bins are marginally less than 3' × 3' × 3', and while a managed pile will heat up in them, it doesn't usually reach optimum temperatures.

A homemade bin is almost always significantly cheaper than a manufactured one. But more important, it can be custom-built to suit your space, materials, and physical limitations. While it's not essential to use scrap materials, you may want your design—in the spirit of composting—to recycle some discarded or previously used wood, wire, or blocks. Bear in mind, though, the material used must be sturdy enough.

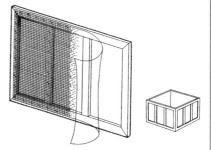

Hardware cloth panels with reinforced strips of wood are a very durable yet lightweight option for compost bins.

It's easy to underestimate the weight of a large pile of moist organic material. It has a tendency to push outward on the sides of its enclosure as it settles, so thin lumber will bow and light wire-mesh cages will wobble. Side panel fasteners must be strong and secure because once the materials are piled in the bin, it's very difficult to repair or replace inadequate panels. If you make panels of hardware cloth, chicken wire, or something similar, staple them securely to sturdy 4" × 4" wood posts. Use heavy-duty staples that are hammered in place (the staple gun variety are not strong enough). Reinforce panels of hardware cloth that are larger than 4' × 4' with strips of wood fastened to the base and sides of the bin.

If you're constructing a wooden box, use either screws or nails. If you're using wooden pallets or pre-fabricated plastic lumber panels, nylon slip straps or tough shipping straps are useful for holding them together at both the top and bottom of each side. They stay tight and are very quick and easy to use.

COMMERCIAL COMPOST BINS

Manufactured compost boxes and bins are available in a large variety of styles, colors, and designs. Typically, they're shipped unassembled, which is less expensive for the manufacturer and, thus, cheaper for you to purchase. Packaging like this also fits more conveniently into your car if you buy it in person. Usually, it takes less than an hour to assemble a commercial compost bin, especially with parts fabricated from plastic, which often snap together easily.

MAIL-ORDER RESOURCES

GARDENER'S SUPPLY COMPANY
128 Intervale Road
Burlington, VT 05401
Phone: 800-863-1700
Fax: 800-551-6712
Customer Service: 800-863-1700
E-mail: info@gardeners.com

PLOW & HEARTH
P.O. Box 5000
Madison, VA 22727-1500
Phone: 800-627-1712
Fax: 800-843-2509
Customer Service: 800-866-6072

SMITH & HAWKEN
Two Arbor Lane
Florence, KY 41022-6900
Phone: 800-776-3336
Fax: 606-727-1166
Customer Service: 800-776-5558
Internet: www.smith-hawken.com/

WORM'S WAY
78500 North Highway 37
Bloomington, IN 47404
Phone: 800-274-9676
Fax: 800-316-1264
Internet: www.wormsway.com

COMMERCIAL BINS AT A GLANCE

NAME	SIZE	PRICE	SOURCE
BIOSTACK COMPOSTER 3 bottomless frames to stack; black polyethylene; hinged lid; extra tier	13 cu. ft.	$99 ($25 for tier)	Smith & Hawken
BLACK GOLD COMPOSTER Recycled black plastic; louvered vents; lid	10.5 cu. ft.	$90	Gardener's Supply
CEDAR SLAT COMPOSTER Removable slats, louvered on 1 side to remove	25 cu. ft.	$75	Gardener's Supply
COMPOST CORRAL Green steel frame for your 1" × 6" × 42" boards; or add their red cedar boards	38 cu. ft.	$50 ($130 with boards)	Plow & Hearth
HI-RISE GARDEN COMPOSTER Recycled black polyethylene; hinged lid, with 2 flip doors; rodent screen; tall and narrow for small area	8.3 cu. ft.	$65	Gardener's Supply
OBEX COMPOSTER Novawood (recycled plastic); expansion unit; blue-gray	27 cu. ft.	$89	Home Depot
WIRE BIN Steel wire square with green PVC finish; lid; pull out corner rods to open side; extension unit doubles space	22 cu. ft.	$40 ($35 extension unit)	Gardener's Supply

While the dimensions of manufactured bins are typically somewhat less than 3' × 3' × 3', properly managed piles will still heat up in them. Temperatures may not reach the optimum heat to actually kill weed seeds and pathogens, but these bins produce compost with reasonable efficiency. They're also adequate for debris storage and simple piles. Although their capacity is somewhat limited, there's no reason why you can't have more than one.

ALTERNATIVES TO BINS AND BOXES

The most difficult part of managing the decomposition process is turning the pile. This process (see pages 34-38) involves considerable physical effort, especially if you have a full-size bin. To address this problem, manufacturers have designed tumbler compost units that remove a large amount of physical effort from the turning process.

A tumbler is designed to aerate your organic raw materials efficiently by rotating the entire composter instead of the conventional shoveling from one bin to another or back into the original bin. Compost tumblers are usually cylindrical with tight lids and air vents. They're made of durable molded plastic or polyethylene. Some are supported by a frame so that they can be tipped or rotated to shift the materials inside. Others are round enough to be rolled.

Barrel tumblers spin on a stationary stand and take most of the work out of turning compost.

These composters generally have a much smaller capacity than a standard-size box or bin, but they turn out compost fairly quickly and can make several batches a season if you have the materials available. Because of their smaller capacity and tight construction, they make ideal kitchen-waste composters. Just prime them with a small quantity of shredded leaves, add garbage at daily intervals, and turn to mix.

ALTERNATIVE COMPOSTERS AT A GLANCE

NAME	SIZE	PRICE	SOURCE
BIO-ORB Recycled black polyethylene ball; 36" diameter; small	23 cu. ft. 13 cu. ft.	$150 $100	Gardener's Supply Plow & Hearth
CAN-O-WORMS Recycled plastic stacked rings 20" in diameter on 5 legs; tap to drain tea from ring	29"× 20" diameter	$100	Worm's Way
ENVIRO-CYCLE COMPOSTER Plastic green or black base; cylinder and lid; turn for compost and tea	7 cu. ft.	$120	Worm's Way
GREEN MAGIC TUMBLER Recycled green plastic; screw-on lid; vent holes; steel frame	6–7 cu. ft.	$120	Gardener's Supply
VERMI-COMPOSTER Black polyethylene worm box; hinged lid; top; 1,000 worms shipped separately	27"×17"×12"	$98	Smith & Hawken
WORMERY Gray plastic, rectangular trash-can style; snap lid; tap at base to drain tea	22 gals.	$100	Worm's Way
WORMERY JR. Green garbage-can style; clamp lid; tap; ½ lb. red worms	5 gals.	$60 ($25 for worms)	Worm's Way

Some tumbler designs feature a moisture collection space at their base. This can be drained to make a compost "tea," a valuable, mildly nutritious additive to the water for houseplants, seedlings, transplants, and even outdoor container plants.

Whatever your situation, there's a composter for you. In fact, there are probably several options for you. As you learn more about this magical process from experience, you will want to experiment with various types of containers and techniques.

COMPOSTING TOOLS *and* SUPPLIES

R egardless of your ultimate goal, the composting process is easier if you have the right equipment. Numerous manufacturers offer a variety of devices that make composting in any style simpler. While it's not essential to have anything other than a rake and a common shovel, various tools can not only ease the physical strain of composting, but help the process take place more efficiently. And as your commitment to composting grows, don't be surprised if your collection of tools grows with it.

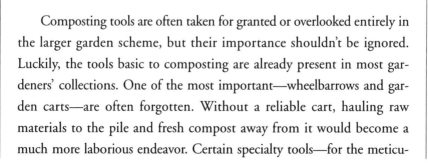

Composting tools are often taken for granted or overlooked entirely in the larger garden scheme, but their importance shouldn't be ignored. Luckily, the tools basic to composting are already present in most gardeners' collections. One of the most important—wheelbarrows and garden carts—are often forgotten. Without a reliable cart, hauling raw materials to the pile and fresh compost away from it would become a much more laborious endeavor. Certain specialty tools—for the meticulous and dedicated gardener—allow you to undertake composting with a certain precision. Sieves and riddles make the task of sifting compost a pleasure. Compost thermometers and various activators allow you to monitor and manage the decomposition process closely. And lastly, the compost fork is probably the tool used most frequently around the compost pile and should therefore be of sturdy construction.

EQUIPMENT TO SHRED OR CHOP MATERIALS

Shredding or chopping organic materials destined for the compost pile offers lots of advantages (see page 27). But before you choose equipment to do this, be sure to consider how much and what kind of yard debris you will deal with over a year's time. If it's mostly leaves, there are several shredding equipment options. Some shredders process dry material easily but cannot handle wet debris or vine prunings. Brush, bark, or pinecones tend to require heavier equipment, which varies depending on

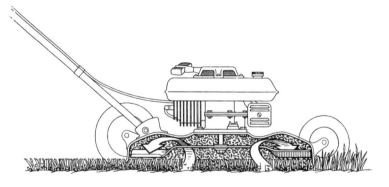

Mulching mowers cut grass finely, which allows you to either leave grass clippings where they fall or collect them for the compost pile.

the size of the branches. If you have a large piece of property that yields enormous amounts of both leaves and branches, you may need a versatile, heavy-duty shredder/chopper. In addition to your shredding and chopping needs, you will want to consider price in your decision.

LAWN MOWERS: Almost everyone with a lawn has a gas- or electric-powered rotary lawn mower. And virtually any lawn mower can double as a shredder in many situations. Besides cutting grass during the growing season, it can be used to shred newly fallen leaves in the fall. A bag option makes collecting debris simple, but a side-discharge mower is perfectly capable; simply mow in a circular pattern and blow the debris toward the middle of an area for easy collection.

Mulching mowers are the best leaf shredders. They're specially engineered with a high cutting chamber and a unique blade that forces the grass clippings or leaves to remain in the cutting chamber longer, so the blade cuts them several times. A mulching mower will chew up layers of leaves on the lawn plus an assortment of small twigs, bark, and even some seedpods. If you plan to purchase a mulching mower, buy the most powerful one you can afford—at least 4 or 5 horsepower or the equivalent in electric power. Again, it's preferable to have a bag attachment to make collecting debris easier, but it's not essential.

STRING TRIMMERS: String trimmers, or "weed whackers," are ubiquitous in many residential neighborhoods. Powered by either gas or electricity, they feature a whirling coarse nylon string similar to heavy-duty fishing line. They cut through tall grass and weeds around fence posts and walls but are not forceful enough to cut through woody vines and stems. String trimmers can also be pressed into service as leaf-shredding devices. Loosely deposit dry leaves into a large trash can, then put the string trimmer down among the leaves to shred them into smaller pieces. Depending on the quality and amount of power you need, trimmers range in price from $60 to $150.

BLOWER/VACS: Electric- or gasoline-powered leaf blowers are quickly becoming a yard-care staple in many residential neighborhoods. More sophisticated versions now offer a reverse, vacuum-power function, which sucks up leaves from around shrubs, ground covers, and lawns instead of blowing them away. The leaves are drawn into a shredding device and caught in a bag that you wear over your shoulder on a strap. When the bag is full, a zipper at the end makes it easy to empty the contents directly into the compost bin. Again, when you buy this equipment, purchase the most powerful version you can afford. Blower/Vacs range in price from $70 to $150.

Leaf Shredders: If your main source of organic material for your compost pile is leaves from an abundance of trees on your property, the most efficient way to shred them is with a leaf shredder. This machine is designed specifically to shred leaves and functions much like a string trimmer. An electrically powered, tough nylon filament whirls at the base of a wide, funnel-shaped hopper, shredding leaves as they are fed into it.

Some models are mounted on a tubular steel frame so the machine can be set at an angle to give easier access to the hopper. This device is usually set over a garden cart, trash can, or compost bin to catch the leaves as they fall through the open bottom. Its greatest virtue is that it handles enormous amounts of dry leaves very quickly—as fast as you can feed armloads into the funnel. Moist leaves shred more slowly. Leaf shredders range in price from $80 to $100.

Shredder/Chippers: If your needs require a shredding machine sufficiently powerful and versatile to handle a steady, generous supply of all kinds of organic materials over the season, then it's worth the significantly greater expense of a shredder/chipper. Similar to the large commercial shredder/grinders used by landscaping and arborist services, this equipment is available in residential size. Various models are designed and powered to handle wet or dry leaves, vines, small branches, pinecones, light bark, straw, dried cornstalks, fruit rinds—almost anything that your yard produces. The largest and most powerful of them will shred limbs up to 3" in diameter, but can't process stumps, heavy chunks of bark, or big branches.

Deciding which shredder/chipper model to buy is not necessarily a function of your property size. A

Leaf shredders can shred large quantities of dry leaves in a very short time.

small property with lots of trees and a big garden will generate a greater variety and volume of material than a large property that has only extensive lawn and a few shrubs. Also, consider that you may decide to run your compost pile through the shredder when you turn it. If this is the case, look for a larger shredder with a generous hopper and wider openings in the discharge grate to prevent clogging. Shredder/chippers come in both gasoline- and electric-powered models. Gasoline-powered versions tend to be stronger and more durable.

SHREDDER/CHIPPER POWER COMPARISON

ELECTRIC	GASOLINE
Small, lightweight	Heavy, sturdy
Less power	More powerful
Easy to move around	More stable
Easier to turn on and off	Needs more maintenance
Less noisy	Quite noisy
Handles woody material well	Handles most material well
Tends to jam more easily	Larger, so fewer jams
Best for dry materials	Handles wet materials
Feeds more slowly, less volume	Handles large volumes quickly
Restricted to electrical source	More mobile

When choosing a shredder/chipper model, there are two engineering issues to consider, and each influences the price of the equipment. The most important issue is power. If the machine is not powerful, it won't be able to process organic material quickly. Less powerful machines are more appropriate where there's a variety of materials, but not large volumes. Heavy-duty machines are the best choice when there's both a large variety and a large volume of materials to be processed on a regular basis.

The other engineering factor to take into account when selecting a shredder/chipper is the chopping mechanism. Manufacturers typically design these machines with two separate hoppers—a long, narrow one for branches and a much wider one to accommodate bunches of leaves and weeds. While every version has blades to chip woody branches, dif-

SAFETY HINTS FOR SHREDDER CHIPPERS

While shredder/chippers help the compost enthusiast, there are inherent dangers in operating them. By nature, they're heavy, powerful, and violent machines that merit the greatest respect at all times. Regardless of the type or brand you ultimately purchase, it's extremely important that you follow the manufacturer's recommendations for proper use.

Never remove or disable safety devices on the machine. The single greatest hazard is flying debris occasionally ejected from the access hopper by the power and vibration of the hammer action within the machine. Usually, the hopper is guarded by a baffle to keep debris in the throat of the hopper and on its way to the hammer. Its dual purpose is also to keep your hands and arms out of the machine. Resist the temptation to remove this device for any reason.

Take the time to dress properly for safety. Eye and ear protection is essential. Even if it's hot, wear gloves and clothes that cover your skin but are not loose or baggy enough to catch on the machinery. Shredding generates a lot of dust, so a pollen mask is also a good idea. Lastly, be sure that your equipment is firmly positioned on level ground before you start it.

Always take the following safety precautions when using shredder/chippers or other power equipment:

- *Be alert. Do not use equipment when you are tired, on medication that causes drowsiness, or under the influence of alcohol.*

- *Do not allow children or pets in the area where machines are being operated.*

- *Wear long pants and long sleeves that are not loose fitting to protect against sunburn and flying debris.*

- *Wear ear protection. Lawn mowers and other power equipment operated for more than 20 minutes cause low-grade hearing impairment.*

- *Wear eye protection to guard against flying debris.*

- *Wear tough gloves.*

- *If you are sensitive to dust, wear a pollen mask.*

- *Keep hands away from the mower discharge vent or shredder hopper. Coax bulky materials into hoppers with a sturdy stick.*

- *Do not operate gasoline-powered equipment in an enclosed space.*

- *Do not attempt to repair or unclog equipment while it is running.*

ferent models may come equipped with either sharp blades or hammers at the base of the main hopper. Most smaller versions of shredder/chippers usually feature some kind of knife device to cut and shred the organic materials. Larger models tend to have hammers. Be sure to consider how easy it is to remove a dull knife or hammer for repair on the models you evaluate.

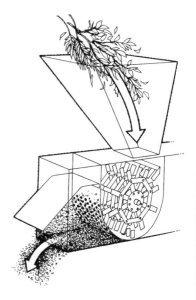

Each shredding mechanism also has certain disadvantages. Knife or blade assemblies grow dull sooner and need sharpening more often, although they tend to be less expensive. Hammers don't get dull, but they wear down over time. Their longevity is doubled if they're designed to be reversible, but they're quite expensive to replace.

Shredder/chippers work by taking material into the hopper, which sends them into a hammer assembly, where they are shredded. Ground-up materials are spit out past a baffle, or guard, which protects the user from flying debris.

HEAVY-DUTY SHREDDER/CHIPPERS: A heavy-duty, general-purpose residential shredder/chipper may cost $1500 or more. However, if you intend to undertake a managed composting operation with a wide variety of both yard and out-sourced raw materials, you may find that this initial investment is well worth the equipment's long-term durability.

Heavy-duty shredder/chippers are available in 5 to 8 horsepower. Their stability, versatility, and durability allow them to last for decades if properly maintained. They can shred or chip enormous volumes of organic materials quickly—a partially decomposed pile 4' × 4' × 4' in size can be shredded in about an hour.

FOOD PROCESSORS, BLENDERS, OR JUICERS: You may already have a shredder for your kitchen wastes inside your home. A food processor, blender, or juicer can double as a shredder if you want to add kitchen waste to your pile or pour it directly on garden beds.

OTHER COMPOSTING TOOLS AND SUPPLIES

In addition to shredding or chopping equipment, there are other tools and accessories designed specifically for composting activities. Some are so helpful that they're virtually essential for simple or managed piles. Others are useful for managed piles but not absolutely necessary for simple piles.

COMPOSTING FORKS: A shovel is not very effective for working with organic materials—neither as you collect them nor when you build and turn your pile. The best tool is a composting fork, which is also known as a "manure" fork and often confused with the "digging" fork. In many ways, the compost fork bridges the gap between the digging fork and the manure fork. It's five tines are oval, not flat like the four tines of a digging fork (both types usually have tines with pointed tips). Unlike the more delicate manure fork, a compost fork can be thrust into the middle of a compost heap and lifted or pulled without bending the tines.

Typically, a compost fork's head spans 9", which allows the user to grab a large amount of materials with each gesture. The head is usually "dished," or slightly bent like a shovel, to facilitate scooping and lifting loads of leaves, wood, chips, twigs, or other organic material. Most important, the generous spaces between the tines in a compost fork allow important organisms to remain undisturbed while air penetrates the pile's core.

While there are many variations that closely resemble one another, the basic steel tine compost fork is a staple for any composting operation.

Compost forks are available with sturdy ash handles, although some have fiberglass ones. The forks come in both long-handled and short-handled styles, and some feature a T-grip or ergonomic handle design. The very best compost forks will have a solid-socket construction—where the handle is riveted into a socket that is part of the tool's head—and can be expected to last indefinitely with proper care. The compost fork is the tool you will likely use the most, so it's important to buy a high-quality model.

GARDEN CARTS AND WHEELBARROWS: If you're already a gardener, you probably have some sort of wheelbarrow or cart to transport plants, tools, and bags of fertilizer around the yard. Once you get into composting, you may find that your cart is not large enough, or that you need a second vehicle specifically suited to hauling raw materials and finished compost. Since the largest-capacity wheelbarrows hold only about 6 cubic feet, their usefulness is limited. But they're handy for distributing small piles of finished compost around the yard. Models with substantial pneumatic tires and rustproof construction are the best choice. Plan to spend between $50 and $100 for a large-capacity, high-quality wheelbarrow.

Garden carts hold about 18 cubic feet and are the workhorses of a composting operation. Their boxy style and deep sides give them balance and the capacity for carrying bulky loads like bales of straw and peat moss. It's best if they have a single tubular metal-loop support running across the back of the cart to balance the front wheel assembly, rather than two separate legs that might sink into the ground with the weight of a full load. Most carts are constructed of plywood reinforced with galvanized metal edges and frame; the more expensive versions use zinc-coated steel. An especially handy feature is the sliding front panel, which is easily removed for forward dumping. The best carts have large-diameter pneumatic tires on zinc-plated, welded-spoke wheels, and a ball-bearing axle.

Lightweight folding aluminum carts are very similar to traditional garden carts. They are both strong enough to carry several hundred pounds and have the added advantage of easy storage. These carts feature large 20" pneumatic tires, a removable front panel, and a lightweight, rustproof chassis.

Another option is a hybrid between the cart and wheelbarrow. It features wheels that can be adjusted along the axle to be wide under the carrying tray for stability or narrow on the axle for difficult terrain or going up planks. It has a painted steel body and 4' × 4' × 4' capacity that expands to 100 cubic feet with an optional mulch carrier. It's capable of carrying up to 400 lbs.

PRUNERS AND LOPPERS: A sturdy pair of quality pruners and loppers—the long-handled pruners that tackle fatter, tougher stems and branches—make preparing organic raw materials for the pile easier. They're particularly effective at reducing piles of brush, twigs, or vines for the compost pile.

Typical pruner handles are made from forged alloy, lightweight graphite, or composite. The best designs have ergonomically styled plastic or cushioned grips to reduce fatigue with long use. Either bypass (curved blades that "draw cut," slicing knifelike though wood) or anvil-type (a cutting blade comes down on a finger-width anvil, like a chopping block) blades are suitable, but the anvil style is reputedly easier for people who lack strength or have small hands. If they have hollow-ground (a special manufacturing technique that strengthens blades and allows them to be sharpened easily), precision blades, they can be sharpened for continued efficiency. And the best brands of pruners offer replacement parts.

Loppers are similar in design to pruners. Their long handles may be made of ash, forged alloy, tubular steel, or fiberglass. Some offer a racheting mechanism that facilitates cutting larger-diameter branches—up to 1½" or 2"—with ease. Anything larger requires a pruning saw and may be too large for a shredder/chipper.

PILE COVERS: Inclement weather disturbs compost piles in a range of ways. High winds dry them out, and soaking rains generally cool them down and make nitrogen materials soggy and anaerobic. Whether your pile is simple or managed, covering it is a smart option. Some commercially available bins and boxes come with lids that solve the problem. However, if you choose not to enclose your pile or if your homemade bin has no lid, then some sort of tarp will do the job. The tarp doesn't have to be fancy, just waterproof and flexible enough to fit generously over the pile. Be sure any poly-type material is UV-resistant and woven with stitched, reinforced seams for longer wear. It should also have grommets or some other feature to help you secure it over the pile. Plastic or heavy canvas tarps are fine; old shower curtain liners are not. Other acceptable alternatives include scrap tin sheeting, corrugated fiberglass siding, or outdoor-grade plywood.

COMPOST THERMOMETERS:

Since managing a compost pile is all about encouraging it to heat up for efficient decomposition, a compost thermometer is helpful if you make compost in the managed style. Typical compost thermometers resemble long oven thermometers. They feature a round stainless-steel–backed clear

The most important attribute of a compost thermometer is the length of its probe, which should be able to reach the center of the compost pile.

dial mounted on a 20"-long probe that penetrates the core of the pile. The dial should be calibrated from 0° to 220°F so it registers temperatures in a hot pile, which should exceed 150°F.

A compost thermometer is valuable at two stages in the composting process. First, it registers that the pile is indeed heating up, confirming that decomposition is underway. If it doesn't heat up in a few days, you may wish to rebuild the pile. Later, the thermometer indicates when the temperature of the pile starts to drop. To maintain top efficiency in the composting process, watch the thermometer until it shows that the internal temperature of the pile has dipped to 100°F. Then turn the pile to introduce more air and get it heating up again.

AERATING TOOLS: If you have a simple pile, there is no need to do anything to it. However, you may want to encourage decomposition by

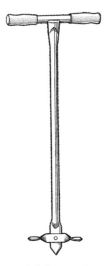

Aerating tools help introduce air into compost piles without the added effort of turning them.

getting some air into it periodically. Aerating tools are specifically designed for this purpose. Basically, they are variations of a 35" galvanized steel rod equipped with cushioned grips at the top and a point at the bottom. Along the rod's lower tip are two hinged flaps, or flanges, which fold up along the rod. To aerate the pile, plunge the rod deeply into the pile, then twist it about one-quarter turn and begin to pull it out again. This motion causes the flaps to open inside the pile, creating air spaces. Repeating the procedure at different locations within the pile fluffs the materials somewhat and encourages decomposition. The design of the handle varies and determines how much pressure you can apply to the tool while inserting it into the pile. While they're easily used on new piles, these tools have more difficulty penetrating settled ones, especially those that are wet.

COMPOST ACTIVATOR: Because the activity of a wide variety of microorganisms drives the decomposition process, more of them will break down the organic raw materials faster. You can increase the natural population by adding good, healthy soil to the pile or by using a compost bioactivator product.

Various products labeled as activator, catalysts, inoculators, or starters for accelerating compost production are available in garden centers and mail-order catalogs. Packaged as powder to be sprinkled on the pile, they contain live bacteria plus enzymes, granular humates, bran or alfalfa meal, or something similar to energize the bacteria in the moist environment of a compost pile. Because the bacteria are live, buy fresh activator each year.

Experienced gardeners often believe that these products are an unnecessary expense. It's difficult to measure and verify their effectiveness because there are so many variables in the materials and construction of compost piles. And there are no standards to accurately measure the relative value of these products. Each company creates its own formula of ingredients and decides how much of its product is sufficient for a single pile. However, research at universities indicates that compost activator or inoculants do in fact make a difference, although it may not be enough of a difference to justify the expense and time to use them routinely. In any case, because Nature provides plenty of microbes that are capable of handling the decomposition job, these products should be considered optional.

There are, however, certain situations where composting activator or catalysts are useful. If the C/N ratio of your pile is unavoidably out of balance—virtually all leaves or exclusively grass clippings, for example— a larger population of microbes will spur the breakdown in the absence of sufficient balancing carbon or nitrogen material. They are also useful where odor is a problem in the compost pile or around garbage cans, outhouses, and trash areas.

Compost Sieves and Sifters: There are only a few occasions when you may want to sift your finished compost to ensure a fine, uniformly textured product. Lumpy compost is no problem for use as mulch around trees and shrubs and among ground covers. In fact, the coarser texture may look better and will certainly last longer.

However, compost should be finely textured when mixed with a potting medium for indoor or outdoor container plants. A topdressing of compost on a lawn should also be even-textured. In these situations, a sifter is a big help. There are commercial sifters available by mail order, and occasionally they can be found at retail garden center outlets. They are also very easy to build yourself from ¼" or ½" wire mesh or hardware cloth. Choose from several types: a hand sifter, a high-volume sifter, and a garden cart sifter.

For those who are planning to produce large quantities of compost, a large sifter frame is the best choice. This can be easily constructed in a 2' square with ¼" mesh. By propping it at a 45° angle to the ground, you can simply push shovelfuls of compost through it and catch the fine compost on a tarp beneath it.

Remember, decomposition is a process that takes place when conditions are right, regardless of whether you have tools and equipment. However, many tools make the process easier, especially for those who are impatient or not as mobile.

THE BENEFITS *of* COMPOST

Using compost generously is the single most important thing you can do for the overall health and prosperity of your landscape. The simple addition of compost to your garden soil, around trees and shrubs, or on your lawn will pay huge dividends in the form of healthy, disease-free plants. And there is also the satisfaction of recycling organic material, the feeling of well-being that comes from physical effort, and the delight found in being outdoors, digging in the soil.

When you mix compost into your soil, the return on your investment from your yard and garden is so valuable that many gardeners refer to compost as "black gold." It revitalizes older plants and invigorates new, young plants. Because there are so many ways to use it, invariably, there is never enough.

Limited amounts of compost usually force you to set priorities for its use in your yard. Decide in advance whether it's more important to use your supply on a new garden bed where the soil has never been improved, mulch new vegetable seedlings, or top-dress part of the lawn that is struggling. Or you can consider several ways to stretch your compost supply by mixing it with materials acquired from commercial or municipal sources (see pages 101–102).

COMPOST BENEFITS SOIL

To make the most of your supply of compost, it's helpful to understand all of its benefits. Compost is essentially a soil conditioner. Adding compost to yard and garden soil changes it fundamentally: Compost alters its texture and infuses it with life to better support plants of all kinds; and compost helps to restore compacted, sterile soil, so it comes to closely resemble the rich natural soil found on the forest floor.

COMPOST IMPROVES SOIL TEXTURE: Because it's light and fibrous, compost aerates any soil that it's added to. Whether you mix it into the soil yourself or let earthworms pull it down from the surface, the net result is more air spaces around the soil particles. It's the nature of these soil particles—especially their size—that determines the texture of your soil.

If your soil is clay, the particles are so fine that they pack together tightly. There is little space for air around them, and the soil feels dense and heavy. The particles stick together when they are moist, and the soil feels gummy. If your soil is sandy, the particles are coarse, larger, and lighter. There is excessive space around them, and water tends to drain through them very quickly.

The amount of space around soil particles affects how well plant roots—especially fine, newly formed plant roots—can grow and move through the soil in search of essential air, nutrients, and moisture. It also affects how much air, nutrients, and moisture the soil can make available to these plant roots. Plants grow well in sandy soil, but the soil doesn't

ANALYZING SOIL TEXTURE

To determine what proportion of your soil is humus relative to its sand and clay components, try this experiment. Fill a quart jar half full with soil taken from several areas of your yard (dig down at least 2" with a spoon). Fill the remainder of the jar with water. Screw the top on tightly and shake it vigorously for 30 seconds or more to thoroughly mix the soil and water. Set the jar on a counter for several days and allow the soil to settle. Its particles will distribute themselves in visible layers according to their weight. The humus will float on the surface of the water.

hold water and nutrients well. Plants struggle in clay soil, but the soil holds nutrients and moisture better. Of course, the ideal soil texture is something in between these two extremes—loam. Loamy soils have ideal

size particles. They are coarse enough to allow space to store air and water, yet they are also fine enough to prevent moisture from draining away. Loamy soils have humus in them, which helps them hold moisture, yet drain well.

CLAY

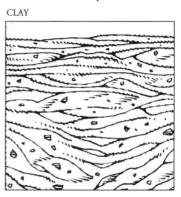

Not everyone is blessed with loamy soil. Compost improves soil by increasing its capacity for holding moisture and draining well. Of course, fresh organic material will decompose eventually in the soil and provide humus, too, but it inevitably depletes the soil of some of its nitrogen as it completes the decomposition process.

SAND

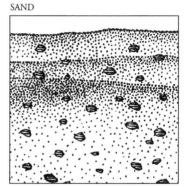

With the addition of compost, inferior clay or sandy soils become friable, or lighter and more crumbly. As they are better able to retain air and moisture, their tilth—a combination of soil's texture and its ability to retain moisture—improves.

LOAM

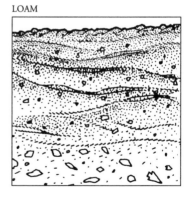

COMPOST INCREASES MICROBIAL ACTIVITY:
At every stage of its production, compost is home to a host of organisms, both large and small, that are responsible for

The density of inorganic components of soil—mainly fine rock particles—and the presence of humus largely determines whether a soil is clay, sand, or loam.

decomposing the organic raw materials. When you integrate compost into the soil, it still harbors lots of these living creatures. They make the difference between live, fertile soil and essentially dead, sterile soil. And they can't live if they don't have humus to sustain them.

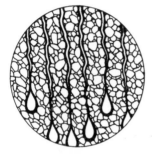

Ordinarily soil untreated with compost (top) uniformly allows water to pass, while soil treated with compost (bottom) encourages water to clump and thereby feed roots more efficiently.

Breaking down chemical compounds bound in the soil particles into nutrients and then converting those nutrients into a form that plant roots can take up is the main contribution of microorganisms. Some are bacteria that convert nitrogen from the air and "fix" it into the soil so it's available to plants. Still other bacteria—more plentiful in compost from simple piles—are organisms that manufacture antibiotics, which attack disease pathogens in the soil. Still other bacteria are expert at releasing minerals from rock particles in the soil. There are also beneficial insects that prey on pest insects and their eggs in the soil.

Microorganisms also play an important role in providing food and air to plants. Plants can use nutrients only when they are in a liquid or gaseous state. The bacteria, fungi, and other microbes in compost reinforce the microbial population already residing in the soil's existing humus. The conversion of nitrogen, phosphorus, potassium, calcium, boron, and many trace minerals and nutrients into accessible gases and liquids is thus accelerated by microorganisms introduced with compost.

COMPOST PROVIDES SOME NUTRITION: Although compost enriches the soil, it is not a fertilizer. Compost breaks down over time into the basic nutrients used by plants to make food, but not in sufficient quantity and variety to make it a reliable substitute for a general, balanced fertilizer. The nutrient content of compost inevitably changes from batch to batch because the raw materials (ultimately the C/N ratio) from which the pile is built vary. The number of times the pile is turned, the internal heat it achieves, and the speed with which the compost is used are all factors that affect the presence and makeup of nutrients in a given batch of compost.

Also, the nutrients compost provides are only indirectly available to plants. Like organic fertilizers, compost depends on organisms in the soil to process its nutrients into liquid or gas form. Compost therefore contributes different amounts of nutrients depending on the organisms found in different soils around your property.

When compost is freshly harvested and has been protected from rain so its nutrients have not leached from the pile, it does contain some valuable soil additives. Fresh compost contributes a measure of nitrogen, phosphorus, potassium, and many trace minerals to any soil. Typically, about half of the nutrients are released for plant use during the first year after compost is incorporated into the soil. Half of the remaining nutrients are released during the second year, and so on.

If compost has been exposed to the elements or stored for the winter, it retains some of the micronutrients even though major nutrients have been released in the form of gases. So, while it doesn't substitute for fertilizer, any compost will improve the overall fertility in soil and remedy a range of mineral deficiencies.

IRON IN THE SOIL

It seems logical to assume that dense clay soils drain poorly and that light sandy soils drain quickly. While this may be a handy rule of thumb, it's not technically accurate. The presence of iron has a lot to do with a soil's capacity for drainage. If iron is present in the soil, the soil will be brownish; if it's absent, the soil will have a gray look to it.

If a clay soil is brown or red rather than gray, it will drain well. If sandy soil is gray, it will not drain well at all. Because compost has some iron in it, it can improve the drainage of any soil that is gray. Simply adding compost to your problem soil can help compensate for the absence of iron.

COMPOST ADJUSTS SOIL CHEMISTRY: Different groups of plants require certain levels of soil acidity or alkalinity to enable their roots to access nutrients in the soil. The levels of acidity and alkalinity are measured in terms of pH, which is expressed as a number on a scale of 1.0 to 9.0, with 7.0 being neutral. If soil tests below 7.0, it is more acid; above that, it is more alkaline.

Acid-loving plants such as rhododendrons, azaleas, and hollies prefer soil to have a pH around 4.5 to 6.5. In contrast, rose of Sharon, but-

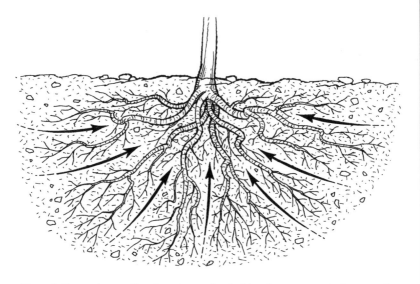

pH can influence how easily minerals are absorbed by plant roots and what organisms live in the soil.

terfly bush, and sedums will accept more alkaline soil that tests closer to 7.5 to 8.0. However, most plants commonly found in residential landscapes do fine in an essentially neutral environment, their soil registering 6.0 to 7.2 or so.

Because the assortment of raw organic materials that end up in typical backyard compost piles usually decomposes into neutral humus, compost does not directly influence soil pH levels. However, it has been recognized by generations of observant gardeners, and more recently by scientists, that compost definitely influences soil pH indirectly in many circumstances. How it does this is not yet fully understood, but researchers have determined that if growing in soil with a high percentage of compost in it (2% to 5%), plants develop the capacity to modify the soil chemistry to suit their particular pH needs in the area where their roots are growing. This is not likely to occur with young, unestablished plants or with annual flowers and vegetables that are in the soil for only a few months. In soil laced with compost over several years, however, some trees and shrubs have exhibited the ability to modify pH levels.

Compost Buffers Extremes of Soil Temperature: Soil temperature is critical to the health and timely growth of plants. Adding rich, dark compost to your soil is one way to alter any soil's response to the extremes of temperature, and to protect your plants or germinating seeds. If the soil temperature exceeds 85°F, for example, root growth ceases until the temperature drops. Used as a mulch in the heat of summer, compost insulates the soil against the sun and allows soil temperatures to stay 6° to 15°F cooler, enabling plants to continue to grow and produce. If the ground is too cold, microbial life is stressed and seeds won't germinate. (In fact, soil temperature is even more critical to the germination of seeds than is ambient air temperature.) For example, no matter when they are planted in late winter, peas will germinate only when the soil warms to 45°F. And the root systems of most plants don't grow until the soil warms to at least 65°F or more. Mixed into the top layers where plants grow, compost darkens the soil and absorbs heat, which stimulates plants to start growing earlier in the season.

Compost Benefits Plants

Whether you're growing annuals, bulbs, perennials, shrubs, trees, or vegetables, they will grow more vigorously and produce fruit, cones, seeds, and flowers more abundantly when they are in healthy, compost-laden soil.

The single most common cause of plant problems is stress. Plants that are improperly planted, don't have the right light exposure, or are in poor soil are vulnerable because their systems are strained by coping with these difficulties—their natural defenses are thus weakened. However, if the soil in which they are growing is improved by compost, the stress is reduced and their vigor improves. They are better able to adjust to problems, and their innate resistance to insect and disease attacks is also improved.

Compost Reduces Insect Pests: In addition to reducing plant stress in general, soil containing compost harbors many beneficial organisms that prey on pest insect eggs and larvae that would otherwise plague plants. Spiders and ants are particularly fierce predators of pest insect eggs. Life in healthy soil maintains a desirable balance among all populations of insects—both predator and prey—so the basic biological diversity is maintained. Compost also adds fatty acids to the soil; these are effective at controlling certain pests, such as root-knot nematodes.

COMPOST FIGHTS PLANT DISEASES: Any ordinary soil contains viruses, bacteria, and fungal spores. They are part of its life. Some of these organisms are part of its decompostion team, while others threaten plant health. The compost you add to the soil contains plenty of microorganisms that combat other microorganisms threatening to plant health. Some of these beneficial organisms in compost also suppress fungal diseases, such as certain rots and damping off, which invade plant roots. These disease-fighting organisms are more abundant in the lower-temperature compost produced in a simple pile. If you have a managed pile, take compost from the outer edges, which doesn't get as hot, for use in disease control.

When used as a mulch, compost also helps control disease in plants. The spores of fungal diseases like powdery mildew are often spread to plants by raindrops that splash up from the soil onto the leaves. A layer of soft, spongy compost under plants absorbs the raindrops, thereby virtually eliminating the spread of fungal diseases.

COMPOST DISCOURAGES WEEDS: Finally, compost has a role in discouraging weeds. Like any organic material, it makes an excellent mulch, even when it's not completely broken down. Spread in a 3" or 4" layer on the soil over plant roots and between plants, it covers weed seeds that need sunlight to germinate. Compost made by the managed method—where extremely high temperatures kill any weed seeds in the organic raw materials from the pile—is best for this purpose.

How *to* Use Compost

The only drawback to compost is that there's never enough. And how much compost you produce largely determines how you will use it in your yard. If you want to top-dress your lawn with it, there won't be much left for any other purpose— no matter how much you produce. Once you make a few batches of compost, you can anticipate how much you will have available and set your priorities accordingly.

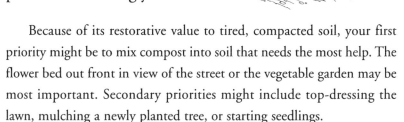

Because of its restorative value to tired, compacted soil, your first priority might be to mix compost into soil that needs the most help. The flower bed out front in view of the street or the vegetable garden may be most important. Secondary priorities might include top-dressing the lawn, mulching a newly planted tree, or starting seedlings.

STRETCHING COMPOST

A fundamental way to make a limited supply of compost go further is to use it sparingly. It doesn't take much compost to bring the humus content of near-barren soil up to 3% to 5%. Spreading a layer ¼" thick raises the organic content of soil by roughly 1%, which is more than adequate in many situations. After all, even poor soil contains up to 2%

humus already. If a soil test from your local county extension agent or a home test (see page 74) shows a minimum proportion of humus in your soil, even a ¼" layer of compost will improve it.

Another simple way to stretch your compost supply is by mixing it with Canadian sphagnum peat moss. Famous for its capacity to hold moisture and aerate soil, peat moss will supplement compost and allow you to use it more broadly. If your managed pile produces about 5 bushels of compost, you can double your supply by adding a bale of peat moss, which is 8 cubic feet, or roughly 5 bushels in volume.

The compost you add to your soil won't last forever, so you'll need a steady supply over time to keep your soil healthy. While it may take two years or more for the percentage of humus in the soil to fall in northern climates, it happens faster in southern areas, where the hotter climate spurs faster microbial activity (compost added to the soil there seldom lasts for more than a single growing season).

SCREENING COMPOST

When you harvest finished compost from a simple or managed pile, it may have an uneven consistency. This is usually the case if the materials were not shredded during production. Lumps of partially decomposed materials are not a problem unless you plan to add the compost to a potting mix where a fine, even consistency is desirable.

Screening compost is easy to do with a sifter made from large mesh screening (½" is ideal) or with one purchased at a garden center. Steady the sifter over a trash can, garden cart, or pail to catch the sifted compost. Throw any lumps and matted leaves that don't pass through back onto the compost pile for further decomposition, or use them as mulch under trees and shrubs.

An alternative to hand sifting is running coarse, finished compost through a shredder. It will acquire the beautiful, fluffy, uniform texture of commercial potting soil. The main drawback to shredding compost is that finer material breaks down faster in the soil than coarse compost. Also, the shredding destroys any worms that reside in the compost.

Using Compost in Your Landscape

When deciding how to make the best use of your valuable compost supply, weigh all of your options. Make your choices based on the priorities of your yard: A newly prepared garden bed is often a prime candidate for soil improvement; a section of struggling lawn benefits greatly from a topdressing of compost; and there are always trees and shrubs that respond well to a mulch of compost. Transplants, seedlings, and container plants are all options for your precious compost. It can even be used as a poultice on wounded trees.

Using Compost in New Areas: One of the most common uses of compost is to improve the soil in a newly established garden bed. Typically, soil under lawn-grass sod or on sites of recent construction is in terrible shape. Builders routinely strip away topsoil at construction sites and drive heavy equipment repeatedly over what remains, so it's both sterile and extremely compacted. When this inferior soil is turned into a planting bed, it needs a great deal of humus in order to support vigorous plants.

More compost is required to build soil than to merely improve it. Begin by laying out the area for a new garden or shrub bed and removing any turf sod that covers it. (The sod can go onto the compost pile.) Then spread a 2" to 3" layer of compost over the area.

A rototiller is a good option for mixing compost into soil over a large area.

With a shovel or hand cultivating tool—even a power tiller—mix the compost layer down 6" to 8" into the soil. It's not necessary to work the compost any deeper; most plant roots reside near the soil's surface. As your population of earthworms grows in the new humus, they will work nutrients down farther in the soil as they travel.

If the new planting area is going to be a lawn, don't assume the contractor has replaced any topsoil that was removed with equal or better soil. Instead, assume the worst and upgrade the soil as described above, so it will support a healthy lawn. This large-scale job is best done with a rented power tiller. Because lawn areas are likely to be several thousand square feet, this project requires enormous amounts of compost. If you are fortunate enough to live near a source of municipal compost or composted sludge, use that to improve the soil for new lawns.

USING COMPOST ON EXISTING LAWNS: Compost plays an important role when you're trying to upgrade the soil that supports a lawn. If you plan to completely renovate your lawn—that is, start from

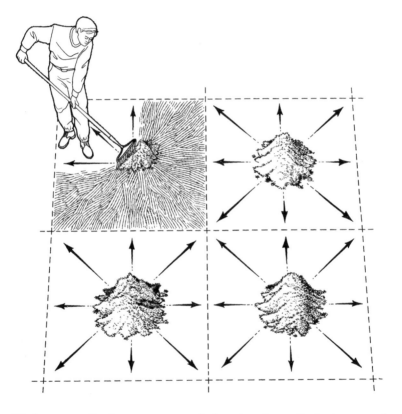

The best way to distribute compost over the lawn is to dump piles in the center of loosely measured areas and spread them evenly with a rake.

scratch with new grass—it's easier to add compost to the soil before you plant new seed. A simple topdressing can also encourage greater vigor from a lawn with listless growth.

LAWN RENOVATION: The first step when replacing an inferior lawn with a new one is to kill off all the old grass and weeds with a safe herbicide like Roundup™ or Finale™. Then spread 1" of compost over the area. If you power-till it into the soil, allow time for weed seeds brought to the surface to germinate, and then kill them with herbicide. When they die, seed the area without disturbing the soil any further.

An alternative method involves aerating the lawn after killing the grass with herbicide. Spread the compost and lightly rake it into the holes created by the core-aerating process. The new grass seed can be sown directly on the compost seedbed. This system takes less work and time, and the compost still gets into the soil.

TOP-DRESSING: Adding compost to the soil beneath existing grass also improves its health and keeps it dense. In the spring or fall, cut your lawn a bit shorter than usual, and spread about a ½" layer of compost over the turf. This topdressing will make its way down into the soil over time, revitalizing it and your grass. If you plan to aerate your lawn, spread compost afterward to facilitate its incorporation into the soil. Earthworms and other soil life will do the rest. The renewed ability of your grass to grow better roots will reduce the time you must spend fertilizing and watering it.

DISEASE TREATMENT: Turf grasses often fall victim to various fungal diseases. Common ones like dollar spot, brown patch, or fusarium patch can be suppressed with an application of compost if they're caught in the early stages. When you first notice the telltale discolored patches, spread ½" of finished compost over the infected area and don't water the area for a few days.

If there is no rainfall for several days, lightly water the treated area before noon, so it has a

COMPOST PRODUCTION RELATIVE TO BIN SIZE

An average compost bin will produce from 10 to 20 bushels of compost each year if it's not actively managed. Ten bushels of compost is enough to spread a ½" layer over about 300 square feet of garden bed. If the soil is so poor that it needs a 1" layer, it will take 20 bushels to cover the same area.

chance to dry off before nightfall, avoiding the dark, damp conditions that fungal spores like. If the disease symptoms persist for more than two weeks, or if they spread to surrounding healthy turf, consider using a commercial garden fungicide product listed for lawns.

USING COMPOST IN GARDENS: Compost is often utilized in garden beds, where its benefits are most appreciated. Its impact on flower, vegetable, and fruit plants is dramatic. How much you use and how you use it varies according to the size of your garden and the current condition of the soil. A good rule of thumb is to spread about a ½" layer of compost over the soil each year if it's in decent condition. In beds where plants have not been very productive and required frequent watering, spread 1" of compost each season for a year or two, then reduce it to ½" each season thereafter.

Spreading compost is easiest in fall, when the annuals have died and been removed and the perennials have gone dormant. Rather than dig the compost into the soil, spread it on top, cover it with a winter mulch such as chopped leaves or straw, and let it sit. By spring the compost will have infiltrated the soil through the activity of its microbial life and earthworms. If you spread compost in the spring, it's best to work it into the soil a bit with a trowel or hand cultivator so it doesn't dry out in the sun.

If you don't have much compost, stretch it by putting it around the plants rather than spreading it over the entire bed. A side-dressing of compost will improve the soil in the vicinity of the plant, and is most effective when it's done in the spring. Lay a circle of compost on the bare soil around the plant stem about as wide as the plant, but don't let the compost touch the stem itself. You can gently scratch the compost into the surface of

DEALING WITH TREE SURFACE ROOTS

Tree roots exposed on the surface of the soil are eyesores and at particular risk of injury from lawn mowers and string trimmers, not to mention potential hazards to pedestrians. Don't try to solve the problem by burying the exposed roots under lots of soil. This will harm the tree and can be fatal.

To cover the surface roots of trees safely, spread a thin layer of a very light soil (a mix of half compost and half soil) over the surface root area. Gradually, as rain pools between the roots, the compost and soil will become integrated into the surrounding soil. Then spread another layer of the light mix. Do this as often as your compost supply permits and as long as it takes to gradually establish a good covering of soil over the roots.

the soil a bit, but be careful if the plant has shallow roots. Otherwise, leave the compost on the soil surface, and let the rain and soil organisms take it into the soil. Target less vigorous plants, and plan to spread compost over the whole area when you have a sufficient supply.

Side-dressing is really a type of mulching, so the layer should be at least 2" thick. Your coarse or partially decomposed compost is ideal for this purpose because it holds more moisture and effectively discourages weeds while it breaks down slowly and enters the soil.

USING COMPOST FOR TREES AND SHRUBS: Maintaining the good health of your trees and shrubs with a mulch of fresh compost is yet another way to use this precious resource. Not only does its presence reduce competition from the surrounding lawn for soil nutrients and water, it also improves the soil in which the relatively shallow feeder roots of shrubs and trees grow.

Spread a thin layer of compost on the soil, then cover it with a 2" to 3" layer of chopped leaves, pine needles, or other organic raw materials to keep it from drying out and blowing away. Provide compost for those trees and shrubs that are already protected by a ring of living mulch, or ground cover plants, by sprinkling it down among the plants.

WINTER PROTECTION: Compost in or on the soil helps reduce tree and shrub stress in winter, especially when they're young or newly planted. It keeps soil temperature from going to extremes as it fluctuates between freezing and thawing, which can heave the soil and possibly disturb tree roots. Evergreen plants—which con-

Dig holes around a tree's dripline—the circle that mirrors the edge of a tree's canopy— and fill them with compost. This will condition the soil for two to three years.

tinue to respire and lose moisture through their leaves in winter—benefit most from a mulch with compost. Its presence allows them to have moisture readily available during milder winter days.

Treating Tree Injuries: Because it contains a host of pathogen-suppressing organisms, compost is useful for treating wounds on trees and shrubs. Damage from storms or wind as well as injuries from yard-care equipment may break the protective cover of woody bark and expose trees and shrubs to infection. Used as a compress or poultice placed directly on an open cut or abrasion, compost guards the area from infectious organisms while plant tissues regenerate and close the wound.

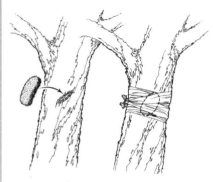

To protect tree wounds from infection, dampen a clump of compost and secure it over the wound with a biodegradable bandage.

To treat tree or shrub wounds, dampen sufficient compost to completely cover the area with a 1"-thick dressing. Press it into a compact wad and lay it over the open injury, taking care to cover the entire area as well as slightly overlap healthy bark tissue around the edges. Secure the poultice by wrapping it with strips of soft cotton cloth or another biodegradable material suitable for bandaging. The tree or shrub will heal in a matter of months, depending on the size of the wound, and you can remove the bandage if it has not already rotted away.

Special Soil Treatment: Certain trees or shrubs on your property may be particularly valuable or fragile specimens that require special attention. One way to boost their vigor and maintain their health is to treat their soil deeply with compost. Give them extra-tender care by injecting compost into holes drilled in the vicinity of their roots. This will fertilize and condition the soil for two to three years.

Drill holes with a heavy-duty hand-held electric drill with a bit or auger capable of making holes 1" to 2" wide and 10" to 12" deep. (They need be only 8" to 10" deep for shrubs that have slightly shallower roots.) Locate the holes every 18" throughout the whole area under the root system of the tree, and if possible, beyond the dripline by 1' or 2'. Then fill the bottom third of each hole with a small amount of slow-acting granular fertilizer and finish it off with compost to the top.

USING COMPOST FOR TRANSPLANTS: If you have only a small amount of finished compost available, it's best used at transplanting time to give plants a healthy start in a new location. While it's no longer recommended that compost or any loose soil be put in the planting holes for trees and shrubs, it's very useful for transplanting seedlings and bedding plants into permanent sites in the yard.

A little compost in and around each planting hole helps young seedlings withstand transplant shock and provides steady nutritional support over the growing season. This is especially important in beds of ornamental perennials and vegetable plants that remain in the same spot year after year.

If you routinely add a bit of compost to the planting hole for every plant you put in your yard each year, you are gradually upgrading the quality of all your soil. Those areas where you repeatedly plant annuals should have especially good soil.

USING COMPOST TO SOLVE NEMATODE PROBLEMS

In some parts of the country, nematodes—microscopic roundworms that live in the soil and prey upon plant roots—are a real problem. The Connecticut Agricultural Experiment Station has conducted extensive research demonstrating that leaf mold composts (compost made exclusively from dried leaves) can suppress populations of harmful nematodes. While many different kinds of partially decomposed leaves are toxic to nematodes, it seems that pine needles are most effective. Mix them into garden soil down 6" to 8" where nematodes are a problem. Do this every year to maintain control.

USING COMPOST FOR STARTING SEEDLINGS: Since it's effective at inhibiting diseases in plants, compost helps protect newly germinated plants from damping-off, a fungal disease that attacks seedlings started indoors. Add compost made at low temperatures (from a simple pile) to the growing medium. A good formula is about one-third compost, one-third vermiculite, and one-third perlite or coarse sand. The microbes in the compost will help suppress the damping-off spores. Once the sprouts appear, be sure that they have good air circulation by setting up a fan to maintain a very light breeze over them.

USING COMPOST IN CONTAINERS: The best planting medium for container plants—indoors or outside—is a soilless mix. Unlike regular garden soil, it's lightweight and free of disease pathogens and weed seeds. It drains well yet retains moisture because it's mostly humus in the form of peat moss. However, because it does not contain any soil, it does not have any nutritional content.

Adding some compost to a soilless potting medium provides mild nutritional support and introduces microbial activity into the root environment of new seedlings, houseplants, and window-box annuals. Add about one-third screened compost to the combination of peat moss, vermiculite, and perlite in a commercial or home-made soilless mix when planting in containers. Because the compost will be used up eventually, just as it is in the garden, be sure to feed plants regularly with diluted liquid fertilizer.

COMPOST TEA AS PLANT TONIC

Compost in liquid form is useful in some situations. Called compost tea, it contains the nutrition of compost but not the bulk.

To make compost tea, fashion a sturdy bag from burlap or other porous fabric. Fill it with compost and tie it at the top so that it resembles a real tea bag. Suspend it in a barrel or pail of water for a few days so it can "steep." The water leaches nutrients from the compost and dilutes them into a mild tonic.

Use this liquid as a soil drench, pouring it directly on the soil at watering time. It is ideal for new plants and very young seedlings that can't handle fertilizer yet. It's also good for watering houseplants and container plants.

Solving
Compost
Problems

Composting is far from an exact science. Even the most carefully made preparations are often at the mercy of chance or timing. Vagaries of weather, problematic power equipment, scarcity of raw organic materials, and limited time are just some of the factors that can undermine a smooth, efficient composting operation. These challenges are virtually impossible to anticipate, but part of the composting process is the satisfaction of solving the "glitches" that arise every so often.

Some problems, however, are so common that they can be anticipated. Most frequently, a range of troubles results from a pile that was built incorrectly. This occurrence is typical for the novice and is usually the case when the pile suffers from low temperatures, poor moisture, or an unpleasant smell. Another frequent obstacle involves recycling organic materials from your kitchen if you have no room for a pile. Last, there is the inevitable problem of insufficient amounts of compost for your needs.

Problems with Your Pile

Whether you have a simple pile or a managed one, there are times when things don't go smoothly. Where you live makes a difference. For example, if you live in a rural area, the smell of the pile is not a major concern because there are no immediate neighbors. Visits by the occasional critter also go unnoticed. On the other hand, tolerance for smelly piles is, understandably, very low in dense suburban or urban neighborhoods where public health and zoning issues are more restrictive. Not all pile "problems" are truly problematic for everyone who composts.

The Pile Smells: The most common composting problem—for both novice and experienced gardeners—is that a pile will suddenly develop an unpleasant odor. This may result from a range of causes, the most likely being that a concentration of nitrogen materials, like grass clippings or weeds, have become anaerobic and are putrefying rather than decomposing. An animal could have died in the pile, or you may have inadvertently included animal products that became rotten. Whatever the cause, the solution to odors in the pile is simple. Just stir up the organic materials in the pile, mixing in some additional carbon material, which injects air into the pile and balances the C/N ratio. The odor usually dissipates rapidly with this treatment.

It's important to mix in brown carbon materials thoroughly. Covering the source of the odor may suppress it temporarily, but it will return unless the putrefying materials are completely redistributed near the top part of the pile. Always keep a bag or two of dried leaves, bales of straw, or hay in reserve, just in case this happens. The problem usually occurs in the heat of summer when carbon materials are scarce. If you have no carbon materials to mix in the smelly pile, Canadian sphagnum peat moss is a good substitute.

If you have a simple pile, odor problems are more likely to occur, since organic raw materials are typically piled randomly as they're collected. Because there is no routine turning or mixing, nitrogen materials concentrate in one spot and become anaerobic. If you choose to enclose your simple pile in a bin or cage, make sure you have convenient access to the top so that you can mix the pile if odor problems develop.

THE PILE DRIES OUT: Both simple and managed piles settle and get smaller over time as the decomposition process reduces the volume of organic raw materials in the core of the pile. Typically, piles settle 20% to 30% over a month or two. If your pile fails to shrink in height over this amount of time, it may be that the materials have dried out, and the moisture-loving, decomposing microorganisms are not able to work efficiently.

For decomposition to take place, the materials need to be moist. In fact, it's a good idea to build your pile with materials that have been out in the rain or dampened down a bit before being assembled in the bin or pile area. Because the outside edges of piles are exposed to air, the materials there tend to dry out between rains and they break down very slowly. This is normal. If you manage the pile, mix them up regularly with the materials in the center so that they will decompose on schedule.

A similar problem arises when the materials deep in the core of the pile are too dry. (They were probably not moist enough when the pile was built.) There is no way for them to acquire moisture from subsequent rains, so decomposition stops. This situation becomes apparent only when you notice that the pile has not settled over time. The easiest remedy for the situation is to insert a hose deep into the pile in several locations, letting it run slowly so that water seeps into the pile's interior.

Another remedy is to uncover the pile—if it's in a covered bin—and scoop out a hole in the top of the pile to trap rainwater for a couple of rains. There is no point in just wetting the top of the pile because the water will run off without penetrating the center. If you manage your pile, turn it thoroughly, dampening the materials in the center as you expose

A simple way to dampen a dry pile is by inserting a hose into its center for a short period of time and then mixing thoroughly.

them, and rebuild the pile. Remember, they should be moist, not soaking wet. Check in a few days to see if things are heating up in the center of the new pile, a sure sign that the microorganisms are back on the job.

THE PILE IS TOO WET: Occasionally, your compost pile may get too wet. This is more likely to happen in simple piles that are exposed to the weather. If there are sticks, brush, and other coarse materials in the mix, they'll keep the pile loose enough so heavy rains can penetrate and soak it throughout. If you leave the pile unprotected, it will decompose even slower than a simple pile usually does, and it may begin to smell. If possible, uncover a layer of the top materials to allow air to penetrate better. Let the pile dry out during clear weather, then throw a tarp over it to block future rains, which would soak it again and set back decomposition even further.

To remedy the problem in managed piles, turn them and add fresh carbon materials, such as leaves, straw, or peat moss. Exposing the materials to the air will dry them out a bit, and the additional dried carbon materials will absorb more of the moisture and prevent the entire pile from putrefying.

THE PILE IS COOL: The internal temperature of a pile is not critical if it's a simple pile. However, if a managed pile does not significantly heat up at its core, there is cause for concern. It should be so hot at its core that it's uncomfortable to hold your hand inside it.

The main purpose of managing a compost pile is to encourage it to get hot and stay hot as long as possible. The constant heat will efficiently decompose the organic materials and produce compost as quickly as possible. If the pile is not cooking at a high temperature—even after you have built it with both carbon and nitrogen materials that were uniformly chopped and mixed together by turning—it may not be big enough.

To achieve maximum internal temperature, a pile needs to approach the critical mass represented by an area roughly 3' × 3' × 3' to 5' × 5' × 5'. A pile much smaller than this does not have enough volume to support the microbial activity required to generate high temperatures. To turn up the heat, add more shredded material the next time you turn the pile so that it increases in volume to the size capable of sustaining the life required for sustained heat.

THE PILE FREEZES: Organisms responsible for decomposition in a compost pile do their best work in the warm weather of late spring, summer, and early fall. They are less active during the off-season when temperatures drop below 30°F. In regions that experience true winter, the residual heat deep in the pile subsides, the activity of the decomposing organisms slows down, and the moisture may eventually freeze.

If your pile freezes, there is no real harm done. The decomposition process just stops. Things will start up again when it thaws in the spring.

To prevent freezing in a simple pile, cover the top with some sort of clear plastic material that traps solar heat and wards off frost. There is a temporary sacrifice of air circulation around the pile, but it's not significant. Alternatively, if local temperatures don't dip below freezing, an insulating layer of material, such as chopped leaves or straw, added to the outside of the pile may accomplish the same thing.

If you manage your pile, you can prevent it from freezing by aerating it. Although you're allowing some heat to escape in the process, the infusion of air and any nitrogen materials available from the kitchen will invigorate the sluggish organisms. Their renewed activity should raise the temperature at the core of the pile enough to prevent freezing.

THE PILE ATTRACTS INSECTS: Compost piles are home to all sorts of beneficial insects and other organisms that participate in the decomposing process. Sometimes, however, piles are visited by pest insects attracted to the rotting or putrefying organic material. Fruit flies, houseflies, yellow jackets, and others are not desirable. In fact, if they're flying around or nesting in the pile, it's a sign that the pile is not properly built or maintained. It is far easier to prevent such infestations than it is to get rid of them.

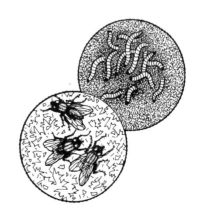

Pest insects are usually attracted by food waste, especially sweet foods like the flesh and rinds of fruits. When you toss kitchen scraps on your simple pile or on the storage pile to await shredding, take pains to cover them well with

The presence of flies or maggots in your compost pile usually indicates that food waste has not been mixed in thoroughly with carbon materials.

BEWARE OF YELLOW JACKETS

In many parts of the country, yellow jackets are a real problem in the summer. Not only do they have ornery dispositions, which often makes them sting without provocation, but their nesting habits are problematic to backyard composting operations.

Yellow jackets prefer to build nests in or near the ground in neglected areas of tall grass or piled brush. For this reason, simple compost piles are attractive to them. The yellow jackets burrow into piles that offer moisture, rotting organic matter, and quiet. Beware of the possibility of encountering a nest if you disturb your pile in late summer.

a good layer of carbon materials, such as leaves, sawdust, pine needles, or something similar. Simply covering the pile with a tarp is not effective against flies.

If you spot maggots, the larvae of flies, you know that you have a serious fly problem; turn the pile as soon as possible. The idea is to have the maggots end up in the center of the pile where the heat kills them.

If you're not able to turn the pile or it's intended to sit in place, you can handle a maggot problem by enlisting the help of natural predators, such as parasitic wasps and predatory nematodes. There may be some parasitic wasps in your yard already, but they're probably not numerous enough to deal with the maggots. You can reinforce their numbers by purchasing more from various mail-order sources.

Predatory nematodes are available from mail-order outlets as well as at your local garden center packaged as a powder activated by water. Spray these microscopic roundworms on the area infested by the maggots and they will kill them in a matter of days. Of course, there are always the synthetic pesticide products, such as malathion and carbaryl. They kill the maggots and break down into their harmless chemical components in a month or two.

THE PILE ATTRACTS ANIMAL PESTS: Because compost piles typically have traces of food in them, various wild animals like raccoons, rats, opossums, and stray cats may frequent the area in search of a meal. Even local domesticated cats and dogs may come around if certain materials in your pile are not mixed thoroughly.

Prevent animal problems by handling garbage properly in and around your pile. Never put meat or meat products on a compost pile. It's easy to inadvertently include a stray chicken bone, a dab of butter, or some gravy with the vegetable peelings and corncobs from a meal. If this happens, bury all garbage deposits on the pile under a layer of carbon material and mix them thoroughly into the pile. Keep straw, dried leaves, or sawdust handy at all times for this purpose, especially if you have a simple pile that's never turned.

Dealing with Kitchen Garbage

Many people who compost don't put kitchen garbage in the pile at all. They often prefer to compost it separately. Because of its high proportion of nitrogen, it breaks down quickly and is easy to handle in

WHAT ABOUT PESTICIDE RESIDUES?

If you plan to acquire organic materials for your composting project from outside your own yard, there's always the possibility that they might be contaminated by pesticide residues. This is particularly true of grass clippings. Homeowners and lawn services routinely spray preventive herbicides and pesticides on lawns. These pesticide residues will contaminate your compost and should be avoided.

The problem is significantly reduced if treated grass has been rained on prior to being cut. This washes any residues off the grass foliage and into the soil, where soil microbes go to work breaking down the compounds.

Try to forage for grass clippings from homes where you know pesticides are not used, or wait until after a generous rainfall to grab curbside bags of clippings for your pile.

Should you encounter pesticides in your compost pile, research suggests that most of those used residentially are broken down during the composting process. High internal temperatures typical of managed piles do the job adequately. Any traces of pesticides that show up in finished compost usually measure at the lowest end of the range typical of suburban soil, which often already contains small quantities of pesticide residues.

several different ways. And there are those who don't have a backyard in which to garden and compost, and may still want to recycle organic waste from the kitchen.

LIQUEFY FOR SHEET COMPOSTING: Nonmeat kitchen wastes can be pureed into liquid form to use in sheet composting. An industrial-strength blender, such as a VitaMixer™, will liquefy even tough rinds, peelings, broccoli stems, and other garbage. Pour the puree directly onto garden beds, around trees and shrubs, and along hedges. Covered with mulch, it causes no odors or pest problems and replaces fertilizer in those areas. Soil organisms will pull liquefied garbage into the soil or you can pour it into prepared holes.

LET WORMS DO IT: Vermicomposting, or composting with worms, is a good way to recycle the family's kitchen scraps (including meat scraps) year-round. Common earthworms are very difficult to raise in a box or "worm farm" indoors, despite what advertisements claim. The

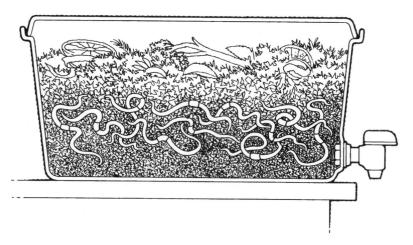

Vermicomposting is an excellent way to easily recycle kitchen scraps and can some-times provide "compost tea."

composting worm, or red worm, is the kind best suited to life in a box in the basement. Because these "red wigglers" don't survive winter temperatures, a worm box is also useful for overwintering some of them indoors until it's safe to reintroduce them into an outdoor pile.

Set your worm box up in a basement, heated garage, or attic that maintains temperatures between 55° and 85°F. The box size depends upon how much garbage you intend to process; if it's too small, the worms will not be able to process large quantities of garbage. Allow roughly 1 square foot of surface area per pound of garbage produced per week; 7 lb. per week needs about 7 square feet of surface area (about 2' × 3½' in area). Make the box from 8" to 12" deep; much deeper risks compacting the materials.

Plan on about 2,000 composting worms (2 lb.) per 7 lb. of kitchen garbage generated in a week. If you produce about ½ lb. of kitchen waste a day, then 1 lb. of worms (1,000) should be sufficient to do the job. And be aware that red worms multiply quite quickly to accommodate any increases in garbage intake.

Provide organic bedding material like chopped leaves, shredded newspaper, shredded cardboard, or peat moss. Add a few handfuls of garden soil to the bedding mix to introduce microbial decomposers into the process. To maintain essential aeration and moisture as the bedding material decomposes along with the garbage, add more bedding material partway through the winter to ensure that the worms have sufficient oxygen to promote their activity and reproduction.

Try to maintain about 75% moisture. Weigh the bedding material and then mix it with water equal to three times its weight. (One pint of water weighs 1 lb.) Be sure the bedding material is thoroughly moistened before the worms are introduced. Cover the worm box with a sheet of black plastic or a wooden cover to keep in the moisture and keep out the light.

Once the worms are established in the box, add garbage to it. Try to follow a pattern where material that has been added to a particular spot remains undisturbed for a few weeks. Garbage doesn't have to be chopped up, but it will break down much more quickly if it is. Finely chop garbage in a blender or food processor first, then drain the liquid, and it will be compost in just a few weeks. And remember to cover all garbage with bedding material.

Renew worm boxes every two to four months by adding new bedding and removing some or all of the finished compost. One easy way to do this is by spreading half of the material from the box, including the worms, outdoors as compost. The worms will die in the cold, but they will add fertilizer to the compost. Fill their space in the worm box with fresh bedding material. Withhold new garbage from the old bedding material to force the remaining worms to migrate into the new material. After three or four weeks, remove the other half of the old bedding, including any worms that might be lagging behind, and replace it with new bedding. The worm farm is now good for another two or three months.

ANAEROBIC COMPOSTING: Kitchen waste can be safely composted in containers that are secure from pest animals. Compost tumblers and compost digesters are examples of this type of equipment. They are not designed to produce quantities of compost as much as they are intended to provide a place to process kitchen wastes

KNOW YOUR WORMS

A whole range of worms is often lumped under the name "earthworm"—the night crawler being the most common. It is important to distinguish between the common earthworm *(Lumbricus terrestris),* which resides in the yard year-round, and the composting worm, or red worm *(Lumbricus rubellus),* which is highly specialized for composting duty but can't survive elsewhere.

Known variously as red worms, composting worms, red wigglers, manure worms, or red hybrids, these worms reproduce much more rapidly than the common earthworm. Consequently, they process more organic material than earthworms do because they increase their population exponentially faster. It takes just 8 red worms to produce 1,500 new red worms in only six months.

Red worms don't usually survive in the home landscape, so they must be purchased each season. There are two types sold: *Eisenia foetida* can't live in the soil at all; *Lumbricus rubellus* can sometimes survive in the soil. Both are good composting worms. A pound of red worms (between 1,000 to 2,000 worms) typically costs from $10 to $12 from mail-order sources.

of all types and keep them out of the municipal trash stream. They usually have tight-fitting lids or covers so that air for the decomposition process is limited.

The small amount of decomposed material that they produce does not have the same consistency as compost made from a mixture of carbon and nitrogen materials in a standard-size pile. Since it's mostly nitrogen-based and is processed anaerobically, it's somewhat slimy and smelly. It is best buried in a garden plot or mixed into a regular pile if you have one.

Substituting When Your Compost Runs Out

Fortunately, there are several alternatives to homemade compost if you are unable to make it yourself. In some areas, local municipalities produce humus products and make them available to residents. Other alternatives are found as close as the local garden center or a neighboring farm. These substitutes are easily used in place of compost or mixed with your compost to extend it for wider use around the yard.

Municipal Leaf Compost: Some enlightened municipalities compost the leaves they collect at curbside from homeowners and then offer the leaf mold product to residents for a nominal fee. Community leaf compost is an excellent source of compost or mulch, so take advantage of it. It also makes a good starter for a pile (if you shred or chop the matted leaves) to be composted further for a finer product.

Municipal Composted Sludge: More than 130 cities in the United States and Canada are composting sludge—the solid residue from liquid sewage waste—into a dark, rich humus ideal for use in residential landscapes. An alternative to ocean dumping and other increasingly unacceptable solutions to a growing sewage disposal problem, composting the liquid effluent from industry and the toilets of private residences produces an excellent soil conditioner. Typically, the sewage is mixed with wood chips to provide carbon and is composted for 30 days. Then it's sifted, mixed with more wood chips, and composted for another 30 days. The final product conforms to or exceeds all EPA standards.

Because it tends to have a higher organic content than compost made in the home compost bin, the value of municipal composted sludge lasts several years longer. A ½"-thick topdressing over a lawn will benefit it for two to three years.

MUSHROOM SOIL: There's another excellent source of humus in areas of the country where the mushroom industry thrives. Mushrooms are grown in a composted straw and manure medium. Once it has supported a crop of mushrooms, it can't be used again for that purpose. "Spent" mushroom soil makes an excellent soil conditioner and is usually available from mushroom farmers at a reasonable price. Allow it to sit for at least six weeks before using it in your garden to be sure the manure is sufficiently aged for use on food crops.

PEAT MOSS AND AGED COW MANURE: A mixture of one large bale of peat moss and one or two 50-lb. bags of processed cow manure approximates the texture and content of real compost. The peat moss provides the humus and the cow manure contributes the nutrients. Because peat moss is a bit on the acidic side compared to the generally neutral humus from composted materials, add 5 to 10 lbs. of lime per bale of peat to sweeten it.

CANADIAN SPHAGNUM PEAT MOSS: Canadian sphagnum peat moss itself is a useful source of humus. It is rich brown in color, with a light, soft, fibrous, and spongy texture. A clean, natural, and organic substance free of harmful salts, chemicals, or weed seeds, it's also biodegradable. It's harvested responsibly from extensive bogs of decomposing sphagnum peat plants in Canada, which are then carefully restored as distinctive ecosystems for the future.

Sphagnum peat moss absorbs from 12 to 20 times its weight in liquid and is also very porous. Again, it's more acidic than compost—its pH testing is about 3.4 to 4.8—so add lime if you are using it around plants that prefer a more neutral chemical environment. Peat moss makes an excellent humus additive to soil and lasts longer than compost. However, it does not have any nutritive value.

INDEX

(Page numbers in *italics* refer to illustrations.)